My Journey
我的經歷

MY JOURNEY - MEMOIR OF A TRUE MASTER

Copyright © 2013 Austin Goh. All rights reserved.
First paperback edition printed 2013 in the United Kingdom

A catalogue record for this book is available from the British Library.

ISBN 978-0-9926151-0-9

No part of this book shall be reproduced or transmitted in any form or by any means, electronic or mechanical, including photocopying, recording, or by any information retrieval system without written permission of the publisher.

Published by Austin Goh Publishing
For more copies of this book, please email:
info@austingoh.com
Tel: 07956898158

Printed in Great Britain

Although every precaution has been taken in the preparation of this book, the publisher and author assume no responsibility for errors or omissions.

Neither is any liability assumed for damages resulting from the use of this information contained herein.

Austin Goh
My Journey

Memoir Of A True Master

London, England
8-8-2013

WARNING

Some of the stunts described in this book are highly dangerous and require a true master of martial arts to guide you. Do not attempt to do the stunts, it can lead to serious consequences.

蛇鶴

詠春功夫

OFFICIAL LOGO

When I reached my 40th birthday, I was asked to write my biography by a few publishers who wanted me to write my memoir. I was then at the height of my career. I was tempted by the fee they offered, but when I thought about it, I felt that I was far too young to write my life story, so turned them down.

Now I am approaching my 60th birthday, so have had another 20 years of life experience in teaching, travelling and healing people all over the world. I feel that now I am wiser and more mature, this is the right time to share my experience with you all.

LEE SHING 1923-1991

勝憑добкун振雄風　李踞興倫揚國術

古干師恩勝公李

This book is dedicated to my Master, without his teaching and guidance I would not have achieved my goal.

Thank you Sifu

No matter how bad life can be there is always a light after the tunnel.
Don't give up on your hopes and dreams, life is what we make of it.

PREFACE

Living in England has its good and bad points but now I understand this is the same everywhere, there is no perfect place on earth; if there is good there will be bad. We are all trying to progress, to improve our lives, and this sometimes leads us to forget why we are here, and instead we focus on material values, trying to overtake each other in finance and power.

But the ultimate goal is to find happiness - we have been searching for centuries for a place where everyone is happy. Where, you may ask, is this place of paradise, of happiness?

In my opinion, it is in your heart, mind and your soul, you just need to find your inner peace by learning to connect your body, mind and soul and work out what is important to you, and then you will have your paradise.

To me, nothing in life is always smooth - there will be some rough rides on our journey as a human being. This is what makes living so interesting, the challenges and the problems we face every day, and how we tackle and solve these — we are survivors and in our daily lives we work to achieve, to overcome issues, and we get through them — that in itself is an amazing feat.

However small or big the challenge is, we overcome it and prevail which makes being human so different. What I am trying to say is, that yes we are trying to live in harmony with each other, and we are the children of Mother Earth and are connected with all living things on earth so we must not forget that not only do we need to live in peace amongst one another, but also with all living things on earth. If we understand and reach a bit deeper into our souls we will live a very full and fruitful life.

There is no doubt that science, medicine and technology have brought us to another dimension in our way of thinking and living how we get on with our lives. But still to me there is no difference compared to a thousand of years ago; humans were also trying to improve their lives then, just as we are doing now, but once in a while someone comes along who changes the way people think.

I think this happened to me with Wing Chun and Chi Kung - teaching it openly and with no complicated movements or philosophy to confuse students or make the teacher sound important; drawing it back to its true meaning and teachings. To me it is not the quantity, but the quality of learning.

While writing this book many memories came flooding back to me, whether good or bad, they have made me reflect and see what I have achieved, and survived - and there were times I felt like just giving up yet I did not. Sometimes it's good to stop and look back; we're moving forward that we often forget to see the milestones we have reached.

Is it the human spirit that encourages us to live and breathe the air around us, and improve ourselves as much and for as long as we can while we are here, or is it the urge to take our lifestyles to another level? Whatever it is remember to seek and connect with your inner peace.

There are many people that have helped and inspired me along the way and I truly feel blessed and grateful.

A journey on earth is not just doing everything by oneself, it is a collective of people that influence you, they might even disagree with you, but we must learn to embrace each and every one, whether it is good or bad these people are the ones that have made me stronger. All the negative feedback I received has made me more determined to better myself. This book was written in mind not just to share my life journey also my martial arts experience and philosophy with you.

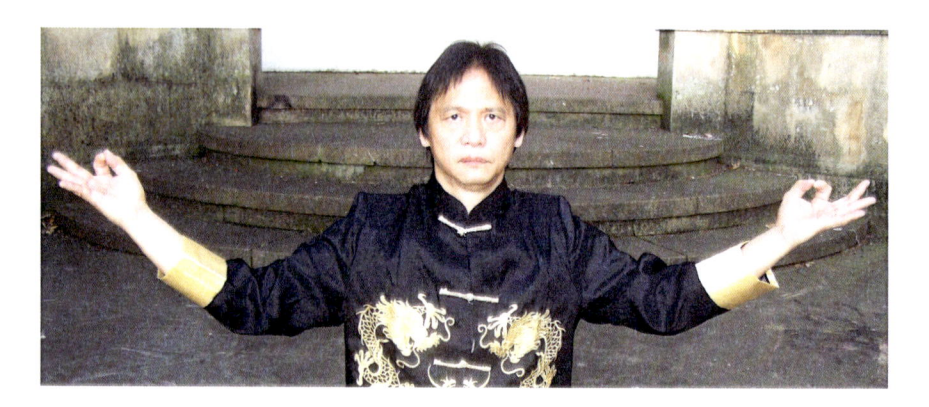

I hope you enjoy reading my memoir. It is just a small journey, one person's struggle to better his life as a human on earth. It might be just a small contribution to send my message to the world but I feel at least I tried.

Finally thank you to my family, friends, parents, grandad, my master and all my students who have inspired and helped me along the way to write this book.

Austin Goh

CHAPTER 1
My Childhood
Journey in London

CHAPTER 2
Meeting Lee Shing
My Master's life history
Grandmaster Yip Man

CHAPTER 3
History of Chinese Martial Arts
History of Wing Chun
Gulao Wing Chun

CHAPTER 4
Training with my Master
Conversation with my Master

CHAPTER 5
Personal training
Student to Master Level

CHAPTER 6
Opening My Wing Chun School
The Art of Breaking

CHAPTER 7
My view on training in Modern Martial Arts
Training in the Art
Achieving Sifu Level

CHAPTER 8
Challenges in the Kwoon
Closing down a bad Wing Chun School

CHAPTER 9
Students who trained with me

CHAPTER 10
Respect is Different Nowadays
The meaning of the title "Master"

CHAPTER 11
Incidents in Sifu's Restaurant
A Problem with the Triad
Meeting the Triad's Boss
Problem with the East End Boys

CHAPTER 12
Working as a Bouncer
Problems with the Maltese
Dealing with 5 guys

CHAPTER 13
Meeting Bruce Lee
Meeting Yip Chun

CHAPTER 14
My Travel
TV's " Just Amazing "
Breaking The Guinness World Record

CHAPTER 15
Bodyguard and Stuntman

CHAPTER 16
Opening my Martial Arts Shop

CHAPTER 17
My Darkest Period
Being Ambushed
Healing from my Master
Human Energy Philosophy

CHAPTER 18
Training Human Energy

CHAPTER 19
History of Human Energy
Principle of Human Energy

CHAPTER 20
Human Energy Programme
Conversation with my Master

CHAPTER 21
Healing Experiences

CHAPTER 22
Success and Failure in Healing

CHAPTER 23
Human Energy Experiment

CHAPTER 24
Some Testimonials

CHAPTER 25
Things I tried but Failed

CHAPTER 26
Dreams, Hopes and Wishes

CHAPTER 27
Acknowledgements

CHAPTER 28
Thinking Back
Final Thoughts

CHAPTER 29
Quotes
My Journey
Memories

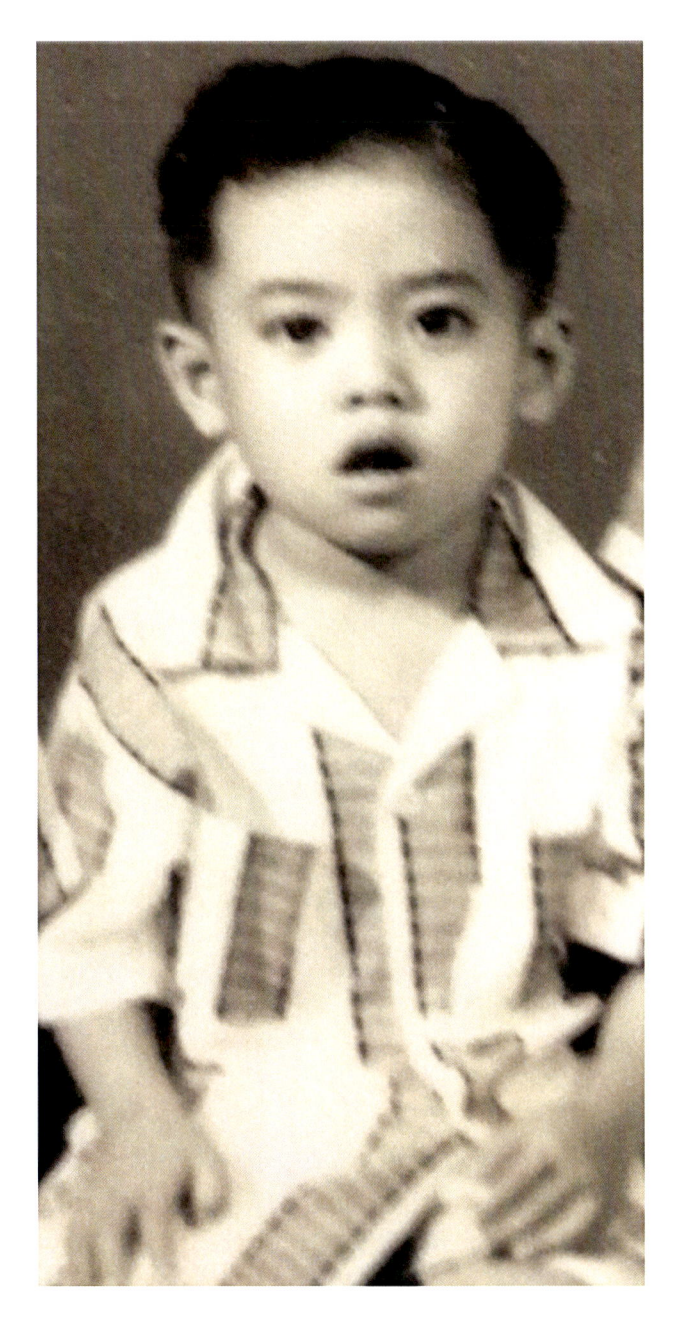

AUSTIN GOH - 5 YEARS OLD

AUSTIN GOH
PERSONAL PROFILE
"The Iron Man of Wing Chun"

Austin Goh grew up in Malaysia where he gained a strong foundation in the martial arts. He left his home town in Malaysia for England in the early seventies to continue his academic studies. It was there that he set up his first Wing Chun school in London and has since expanded into Europe. Austin has also travelled extensively around the world giving demonstrations and lectures in Hawaii, Japan, Hong Kong, Thailand, Malaysia and Singapore.

Austin Goh was taught Wing Chun by his Master, Lee Shing. Austin was a closed-door student and spent many years training with his master. Now Sifu Austin Goh is the only successor to be still teaching the Lee Shing Lineage which includes centre line Wing Chun, Gulao Wing Chun and Dai Lim Tao.

MALACCA IN 1954

Austin's success as a teacher in the martial arts is due to his friendly and open-minded teaching methods which have gained him the respect and loyalty of his students. He teaches that anyone who wants to succeed in any martial art must be prepared to work hard and be determined to achieve this goal, and he leads in this respect by his own example.

Austin was the first Malaysian Chinese Wing Chun teacher in Europe to teach not only Bil Chee (Wing Chun's third form) but also the Pole form, Wooden Dummy form, and the Butterfly Knives. Austin feels that there should be no secret formulas or techniques in any style of martial art. He believes that as times change, so must the arts — what worked 300 years ago might not be practical now, and so the training systems and principles must change to suit our modern life. For anything to survive, it should be taught openly and properly.

In 1984 Austin appeared on the British television programme "Just Amazing" where he gave a chi demonstration. In an awesome display of chi strength, he set a new world record by having fifteen four-inch concrete blocks broken on his chest with a sledgehammer wielded by one of his students.

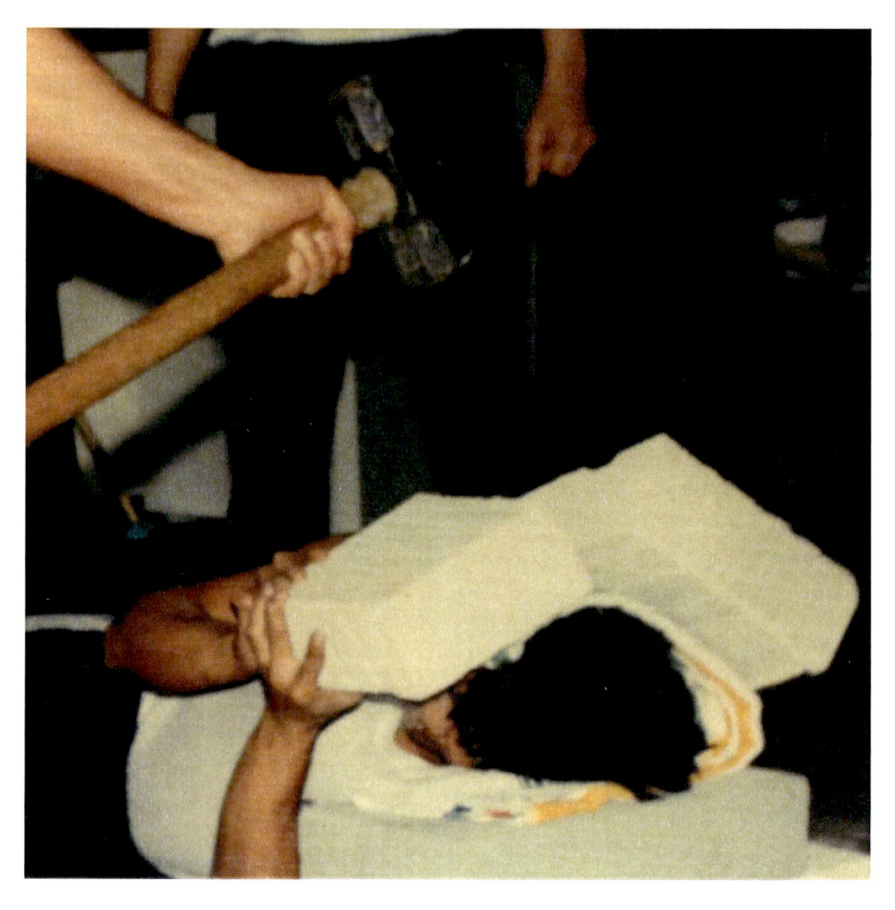

He also stunned the audience by having two concrete blocks placed against the side of his head while lying on the floor, then the student broke the blocks with a sledgehammer!

After this performance, the audience nicknamed him the "Iron Man of Wing Chun". He is also a Guinness record holder for breaking concrete blocks with his bare arms in 2001.

My Journey - 我的平生經歷

YOUNG AND READY

THE WOOD HORSE
1954 AND 2014

The year of the Horse: is a time for progress, it is a very happy-go-lucky, frantic and wild year that is both adventurous and satisfying. There will be an upward turn to the year with a deal of good humour. It is a year for going it alone, perhaps with some shocks in store but on the whole a courageous and daring year.

In Chinese astrology, people born during the Year of the Horse have a pleasant, amiable, easy going disposition which guarantees popularity and a large following of friends. Blessed with good humour and geniality, they are extremely comfortable to get along with for they have the knack of instantly putting people at their ease.

Charming and cheerful, the Horse is an extremely likable character. Hard working, self-possessed and sharp, the Horse skillfully acquires power, wealth and respect. However, the Horse's sometime-appreciated frankness can be tactless. In truth, they are more cunning than intelligent, and they know it.

INTRODUCTION

According to Chinese astrology, I was born in the year of the horse - in the state of Malacca in Malaysia on September 10th 1954 to my mother Chung Ooi Mooi and my father Goh Ah Sang. I am a second generation Chinese born in Malaysia.

As a child I was always sick and weak so my mum took me to many so-called healers in temples, in order to improve my health. This was a very common thing to do in the 50s and 60s. I was taught a few breathing exercises by the Taoist priest in the temple.

It was a life changing experience - my health improved greatly and I began training in energy work whenever I could. I felt stronger and moved on to martial arts training, the Shaolin Wing Chun system and energy work with my uncle.

I entered many full contact tournaments at the age of 16, knocking out most of my opponents from different styles and even organized some street bare knuckles fights to earn extra money for my trip to England. Most of my opponents were knocked down with my Wing Chun punches, so after that they nicknamed me "the boy with the iron fists."

MALACCA TEMPLE 1959

JOURNEY TO LONDON

At the age of 18 in 1972 I decided to come to London to further my studies in Physical Education and English, luckily I was sponsored by my English uncle Chris Blackmore who was married to my Auntie Chiu.

After two months living with them in the army barracks in Maidstone I had to go to London to start my studies in Woolwich College.

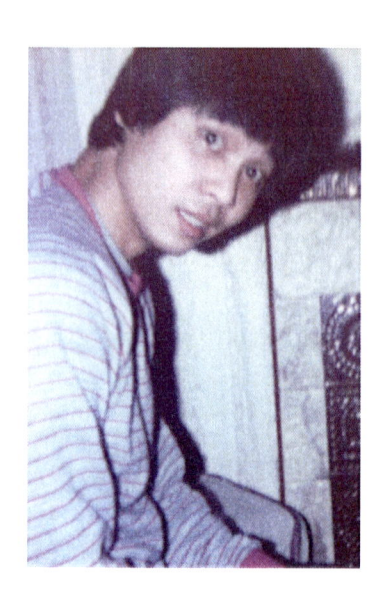

In order to have a few extra pounds for my studies and expenses I decided to look for different ways to earn some money, so I taught Wing Chun kung fu to a few friends, just to earn a bit of pocket money to pay my bills.

And in the evening I worked as a bouncer in a night club called "Le Kilt" in Greek Street, Soho; after finishing work in the club most nights I would normally go to have my supper in London Chinatown's Canton restaurant which was the only place that was open till the morning.

LONDON 1972

CHAPTER 1
MY CHILDHOOD

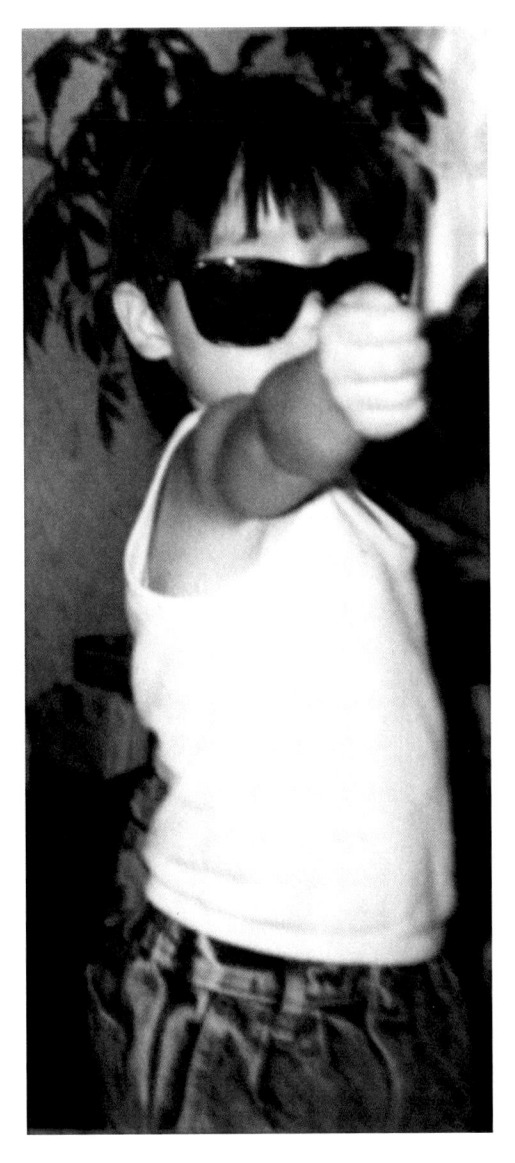

Let the Journey Begin

MY CHILDHOOD

When I was 7 years old my father decided to take on another wife, my mother was horrified and angry. She had given him 3 sons of which I am the second. My grandfather was a very wealthy land owner who bought up a lot of land in Malacca. In those days a man could have two or three wives, especially if he was rich. This was very common in the 50s.

My mother was so upset and warned my father that if he went ahead and took on another wife, she would leave him. But in those days women were treated badly, especially in eastern culture.

My grandfather himself had 2 wives because of his wealth. What still amazes me is that they all lived together; me, my grandfather and all grandmothers, aunties, uncles, cousins and brothers - it was great and I was never bored when at home.

During dinner time we all had to sit and wait for my grandfather as he was the king of the house. No one dared to start eating until he had sat down. We also had to wait for our first grandmother who had bound feet restricting her from walking properly.

At that time I was too young to understand all this, now I resent that thinking. My mother was heartbroken but still insisted that if my father took on another wife she would leave him and take all three sons with her.

My grandfather intervened and told my mother to go if she wanted and never come back She told my grandfather that she wanted to take her children with her. My grandfather said that she could only choose one of us.

For whatever reason it was she chose me. After many years I asked her why did she choose me and she said that I was always a very happy child, never complaining even when sick. It must of been heartbreaking for her to choose me and leave my two brothers behind - how she did it is beyond my imagination.

We went to live in my first auntie's house and it was a tough time for my mother but she never complained and just wanting to give the best to me.

Being 7 years old, I always wanted to have my own goldfish which I could not afford to buy. My next door neighbour's son had a few in his aquarium - so thinking to myself that if I went over and take one they might not notice it. I climbed over and managed to catch one and put it in my aquarium.

Unfortunately for me, the son realised that one of his goldfish was missing and asked around. My auntie found it in my room. She was so angry saying that I was a thief and had disgraced the family making them lose face to the neighbours.

She grabbed my arm and hit me with a cane - it was so painful I can still remember it now. Her beating went on and on until she was exhausted. My body, legs and face were covered with bruises and marks had appeared all over me - I was horrified.

Thinking about this makes me wonder how some people can treat children in this way. Did I deserve this beating from my auntie? She was not even my mother, I hated her so much after this beating and it was just the beginning of my punishment living under her roof.

She told my mother what I had done and insisted that I must kneel down all night in front of my great grandfather's altar to say sorry for making the family lose face.

I fell asleep in the middle of the night as the pain from my body and face was unbearable. I had to sleep on the marble floor with no shirt on and it was so cold. I fainted thinking that I had fell asleep. My mother woke me up and carried me to bed, I was still crying non stop and asked her why she let my auntie beat me like this. She said that she shouted at my auntie but we had to stay in her house and if we upset her she might throw us out and then we might not have a place to go.

I told her I was sorry for stealing. She said stealing is bad if we cannot afford to have things that we want, we must learn to live without them.

My auntie stopped me from going to school for two months until my bruises were completely gone. After that I moved to my third auntie's home, she was so different from the first one, kind and loving and I lived there until I decided to come to England.

Looking back at my past experiences, I think to my self that no matter what happens I will always make sure all my children are well looked after - not having to go through what I had gone through, I still have nightmares about it - it was truly damaging.

This photo was given to me last year from my mother. It is the only memory she had with all her three sons together. 52 years ago and I will treasure it forever.

Early Days

Full of Dreams 1972

JOURNEY IN LONDON

Arriving in London as a young man of eighteen was a life changing experience. Fortunately I speak fluent English as Malaysia was under the British Empire until 1957, and all education was conducted in English until 1969 and it still remains an active language. Certainly speaking and writing English fluently helped me to settle down in the UK a little more easily.

Coming from a hot tropical country, what I was not used to was the cold winters. I had a hard time in the winter, but luckily I had learned the hard chi kung which I practised to keep me warm. It can be very difficult and lonely for someone who has come to a strange land with no friends and family to go to, if you ever needed help.

Nevertheless, I persevered and got on with it; going to college and looking for odd jobs to support me. I rented a small bedsit in Finsbury Park which was affordable, at that time it cost around £4 a week. The first job I did in London was washing dishes in the kitchen - it was hard work. I never had to work in my life while I was in Malaysia with food and shelter provided, I just went to school and studied.

All that time when I was dreaming of coming to London - I never expected or thought about the reality of looking after oneself, away from family and alone in the real world. It was completely different - people could be nasty and sometimes, I faced racism which I had never experienced before. I had been brought up in a multicultural society where we had Chinese, Malay, Indian, Eurasian and English living alongside one another.

As a child I visited friends who celebrated different religions and festivals - there was no such thing as who or which culture or race is better, and in school we mixed amongst each other as friends- no doubt we had our differences, but not as a race issue, just as people.

I had never been called a "chinky" or "slant eyes" in my life, yet in London it was a common thing to hear. I was feeling lonely and sad and not knowing what to do, some of these people who abused me verbally were big - much bigger than me, yes I had brawls in Malaysia, but the people I faced were around the same height and size as me - I am around 5 feet 7 inches - average in Malaysia, but small among the westerners. I was frightened and tried to run away when faced with it.

This was not me, I usually like to face up to confrontation and deal with it, but what could I do, I was on my own in London with no family or friends close by to give advice and help. I felt such a desire to go back to Malaysia, but thought if I did I would be a quitter, which I could not be so I put my head down and got on with it.

I came really close to going back to Malaysia following quite a nasty incident one evening when I was walking back home. I was confronted by four men who started racially abusing me, calling me names and telling me to go back to my country. I tried to run away but they cornered me to give me a good beating. I was so scared and quickly racked my brain for survival, my uncle's teaching came to me - in order to defend against multiple attackers when you think you do not stand a chance, run as fast as you can towards the weakest one and push him out of the way, and keep on running and never look back.

I took a deep breath and picked the weakest one, quick as a flash, I dashed towards him; my sudden charge towards him caught him by surprise so I was able to push him away and he fell to the ground — this gave me an opening to run, and I kept on running. Behind me I could hear them shouting and they had started to chase after, but I was too fast for them — I ran and ran. I turned my head to see if they were still chasing me, and when I saw that it was safe, I just dropped to the ground with exhaustion.

My heart was beating so fast and I asked myself "What am I doing in this country?" I never expected this before coming here. I studied the British Empire and the great things they did and I admired their culture yet the reality was not quite like it was portrayed in the books. I was very emotional, my adrenalin pumping, suddenly the tears fell from my eyes, I felt sorry for myself, questioning myself - do I need to take this and carry on living in London, or just go home to my family?

I was sitting down on the ground for hours not knowing what to do. Eventually I stood up and went back to my bedsit, went to sleep hoping that when I woke up it would just all be a bad dream, but it wasn't a dream. It was reality. The next day when I woke up I felt frustrated and angry so I went to the gym and punched and kicked the bags with all my strength to release all my frustration, anger and confusion. Blood was coming out of my knuckles yet still I carried on, one of my friends saw what I was doing to myself and came over and finally stopped me.

I was so upset; I felt lonely and afraid, but also, because of my ego, I had never run away from a fight before, this was the first time. I thought I would have rather died than run away, but thinking back I was so young and naive to think like that. If I stayed and took on those people I think I would have been killed or crippled by them and I didn't really want that. It took me a few months before I was able to walk down the street in the evening, and I carried a pair of telescopic nunchaku wherever I went, so that I was well prepared, just in case.

Later I found a job in a restaurant. Working in there was a back-breaking experience as I finished college around 4pm and rushed to work to start at 5pm. It was an Italian restaurant but one of the chefs was from Hong Kong and he turned out to be quite a nasty man, throwing his weight around, especially with me; I had to clean the toilets, wash dishes, I was given every menial job, you name it, I did it - and in those days, I was paid £10 a week.

I asked myself again what am I doing in England, deep inside me these thoughts would go round and round. I now realise how hard is it to make a living in the real world and that I was just starting out. I am not a quitter, so maybe these experiences toughened me and made a man out of me. After two weeks I had had enough, I found this abusive environment did not suit me so I left. In my mind, I always thought that people were always nice and kind, but I met so many bad people, I knew this not to be true any more, or maybe it was just bad luck.

After that I went to work as a cleaner in a big office in Oxford Street and the working hours were flexible; I worked four hours in the evening from 6pm to 10pm. There I met a great elderly Irish man called Tom who looked after me, treated me like his son and helped me whenever I needed it. So I discovered there are good and bad people everywhere. It is just luck or fate, who you meet and when.

I stayed there for three months, then I left and kept in touch with Tom until his death, some years later. That was the first time I ever went to a funeral - it was very emotional to me as we had built up a good friendship all those years, so it felt like losing one of my close family members.

In such a short period of time I had faced racism, prejudice, nearly being beaten a few times - what a tough life, I said to myself. However, I had survived so far so I must carry on, I thought there must be a light at the end of the tunnel, there must be a purpose.

I am not a quitter and I never will be. As the Chinese proverb says... In order to succeed one needs to taste the sour first, then sweetness will come. This was certainly the case. Soon after, a Bruce Lee movie came out and suddenly everyone wanted to learn martial arts so I started to teach to a few friends to earn some extra money so that I didn't need to work for anyone again. I earned enough to pay my rent and food and even my college fee. I told to myself this is better than working in the restaurant or cleaning offices. I felt better, more positive about my future in the UK.

I told my students that I am not a Master just an instructor; as I was far too young to be called a Master. But I hoped that one day I would be.

Teaching martial arts was another learning and challenging journey in my early life. People were all much bigger and physically stronger than me and some of them could be very aggressive; trying to put my skills and my fighting ability to the test. So I decided to increase my physical body strength and power through weights and bag work every day, and instead of taking a bus home I ran back to improve my stamina. It helped but I felt that I needed a true Master to guide and teach me, to show me the right path in my quest for martial arts perfection.

Luckily one of my friends introduced me to some work as a bouncer in a French disco in Greek Street, Soho to help me to earn some extra money. After work I would go to the Chinese Canton restaurant for my supper and it was in there that I met my Master; as the saying goes, the rest is history.

When destiny crosses your path no one can stop it.

CHAPTER 2

Meeting Lee Shing

My Master's Life History

Grandmaster Yip Man

MEETING MASTER LEE SHING

In that restaurant one morning when I went downstairs I saw a man teaching Wing Chun in the kitchen. I later found out it was Master Lee Shing.

I approached him and explained to him my background in Wing Chun and he seemed to know about the different Wing Chun systems in China that were lost after the cultural revolution.

It was fate or luck that we met but he decided to take me as his official disciple which was unheard of at that time, when Chinese Martial Arts were rarely spoken of, or taught, as the communist regime was still feared, even though it was thousands of miles away.

Westerners always thought that the Chinese were very secretive but they did not realize what the Chinese had left behind - often all their loved ones - and what they had gone through in order to keep their lives while fleeing the country from the communist regime.

MASTER LEE SHING

He was the European and UK President of the Yip Man Martial Arts Association and founder of the International Lee Shing Wing Chun Martial Arts Association. He was also a member of the Hong Kong Kowloon Chinese Medical Association and was a qualified Chinese doctor. These positions are testimony to a lifetime's dedication to Wing Chun and his impact on the development of Wing Chun in Europe, which has been very significant and yet it is largely an untold story.

Master Lee Shing was born in 1923 in Hoxan in Southern China. He first studied Gulao Wing Chun at an early age in mainland China under his first teacher Fong Yee Ming, who himself had learnt from Wong Wah Bo who had learnt from Leung Jan.

Lee Shing was inspired to research the different styles of Wing Chun, he therefore researched and went on to study under Fung Sang who was one of the central figures of Wing Chun, having studied under his father Fung Lim and his uncle Koo Siu-Lung (both students of Wong Wah Bo). He then went on to learn from the famous Kung Fu Master Ng Jung. Lee Shing moved to Hong Kong where he met and became friends with two Wing Chun experts, Lok Yiu and Jiu Wan. They were two of the four leading practitioners of Wing Chun in Hong Kong who became known in Wing Chun circles as the "Four Kings of Wing Chun". The other two were Leung Sheung and Tsui Shan Tin. It was not long before an exchange of styles took place between Lee Shing, Lok Yiu and later Jiu Wan.

While they were working together one day, an older gentleman entered wearing the traditional Chinese dress. Lee Shing noticed that the others greeted the man very respectfully, so much so that he was curious to know who he was. It was then that the stranger was revealed to be none other than Grandmaster Yip Man, the teacher of the "Four Kings" of Wing Chun; in fact Lok Yiu, a former master of another kung fu style, was Grandmaster Yip Man's first student in Hong Kong.

Lee Shing was formally introduced by Jiu Wan to Grandmaster Yip Man. At the time Grandmaster Yip Man was teaching Wing Chun in Hong Kong's Restaurant Workers" Union. Lee Shing was fortunate enough to be accepted by Grandmaster Yip Man as a student and received instruction privately from him on a one-to-one basis. He was known only to Grandmaster Yip Man's senior students and later to Grandmaster Yip Man's eldest son Yip Chun. Over the years, Lee Shing learnt the complete Wing Chun system. He had mastered the three hand forms, the Wooden Dummy form, the Six-and-a-Half Point Pole form and most importantly of all, Grandmaster Yip Man had taught Lee Shing the complete Butterfly Knives form and its applications.

This last form was of particular importance as it represented the highest point of learning in Wing Chun. At the time Grandmaster Yip Man had taught only three people the complete knives form. Lee Shing was allowed to open up a school on Hong Kong Island in the early 50s - with the opening ceremony being conducted by Grandmaster Yip Man himself.

It was at this time that Lee Shing met Yip Chun who had resumed his studies in Wing Chun. The two became firm friends and henceforth when Yip Chun came to England, he would always stay at Lee Shing's home.

Master Lee Shing brought Wing Chun to Europe and was a major influence on the development of Wing Chun in the western world. For many years Master Lee Shing had a close friendship with Master Yip Chun, eldest son of Yip Man.

There was great mutual respect on both sides. After Yip Chun's arrival in Hong Kong from China they were introduced in the famous Yang's restaurant by Grandmaster Yip Man. Whenever he visited the UK Master Yip Chun would visit Master Lee Shing and stay in his house as an honoured guest to discuss amongst other things the further promotion of Wing Chun in the UK and Europe.

Though he was always one to shun the spotlight, Master Lee Shing should be given full credit for bringing the Chinese Martial Art of Wing Chun to the United Kingdom and Europe. Thanks to him, I have been able to spread the art all over the world.

GRANDMASTER YIP MAN

Grandmaster Yip Man was born in the year 1898 in the town of Fatshan in Kwangtung Province, in Southern China to a wealthy merchant family. The Yip family permitted Wing Chun master Chan Wah Shun and live there to teach a small group of disciples in the family temple, since Chan's local reputation as a fighter discouraged thieves and highwaymen from attacking the family businesses.

Yip Man would watch Chan Wah Shun drill his disciples in the ways of Wing Chun. Soon the boy's visits became more regular until, Yip Man was about nine years old he approached Chan and asked to train under him

He studied with Chan Wah Shun for five years, until the old master's death. Yip subsequently spent another two and a half years training with his senior, Ng Chung So. When Yip was 16 years old, his parents sent him to Hong Kong to attend St. Stephen's College. There, he quickly fell in with a clique of classmates who liked to offer and accept kung fu challenges. He welcomed the opportunity to put his Wing Chun training to the real test.

One evening Yip Man met a elderly man living on a fishing boat anchored near the typhoon breakers in Hong Kong Bay. They became friends and he performed the entire basic Siu Lim Tao form of Wing Chun to him.

After that the old man agreed to a match. He promptly attacked him but was easily defeated falling into the water. After repeated attempts and repeated soakings, he wanted to learn from the him and soon found out that the old man was Leung Bik, his kung fu elder uncle. who later explained the difference in his Wing Chun compared to Chan Wah Shun's and proceeded to take Yip Man as a student. Yip Man studied with Leung Bik for three years.

He later returned to Fatshan and told his seniors about the old man that he had met. When his seniors scoffed at him, he challenged them and defeated them with his newfound knowledge. later he stayed in Fatshan where he was involved with the police works and raised a family. In 1948 Yip Man fled to Hong Kong during the cultural revolution

In Hong Kong, a homeless and penniless Yip Man was given refuge at the Restaurant Worker's Association, where he taught Wing Chun to the workers until his death in 2nd December 1972.

His most famous student was Bruce Lee who popularised his Wing Chun to the world via his movies.

GRANDMASTER YIP MAN 1873 - 1972

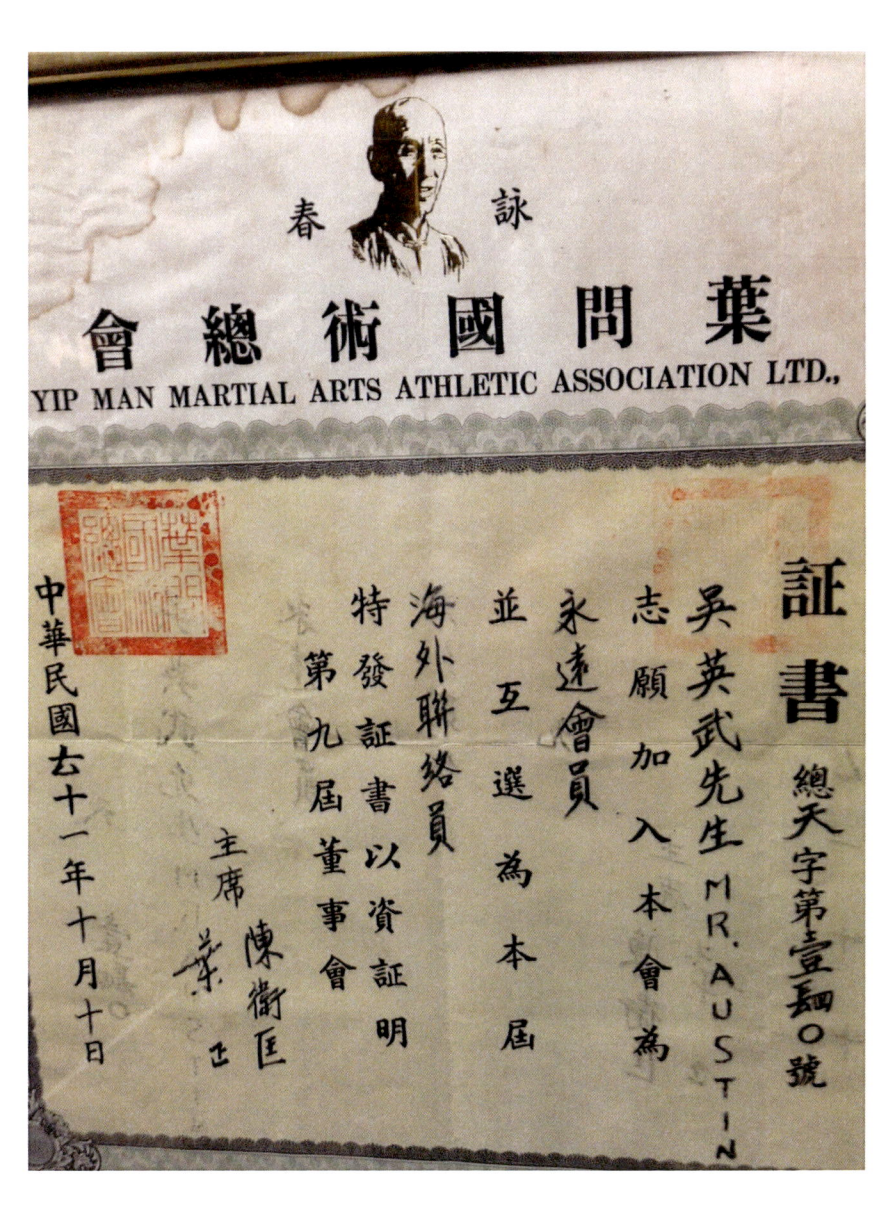

REPRESENTATIVE SINCE 1978

CHAPTER 3

History of Chinese Martial Arts
History of Wing Chun
Gulao Wing Chun

HISTORY OF CHINESE MARTIAL ARTS

Chinese martial arts recorded history dates back to around 525 AD, during the Ching dynasty. The man credited with introducing martial arts to China is said to be an Indian monk name Bodhidarma. 506 —556 AD.

When he arrived in the Shaolin Temple he saw that most of the monks were weak and often fell asleep during meditation so he devised a set of "18 movement exercises based on breathing techniques" - also known as the "18 breathing hands" exercises, which we know as chi kung nowadays.

He taught these to his disciples in the Shaolin temple, believing that by practising these regularly the monks would cultivate health, vitality, and mental clarity, and that would prevent the monks from falling asleep and help them to be physically stronger.

The techniques were formed and developed in mountains in the Himalaya, through daily practice of these techniques its strengthened and improved the health of the monks.

From these form of exercises new martial arts systems, such as Wu Shu, Shaolin Kung Fu, Tai Chi, Chi Kung and Wing Chun were developed and continued to flourish throughout China.

At that time China was ruled by the Ching Dynasty. Perhaps the best-known story of the Temple's destruction is that it was destroyed by the Ching Emperor for supposed anti-Ching activities in 1732.

This destruction is also supposed to have helped spread Shaolin martial arts throughout China by means of the five fugitive elders monks who fled the temple when it was burned down. The five monks are known as the venerable five. The Shaolin 5 Elders are Jee Shin, Bak Mei, Fung Do Duk, Miu Hin and Ng Mui.

SHAOLIN TEMPLE - BIRTHPLACE OF WING CHUN

HISTORY OF WING CHUN

Ng Mui is credited as the founder of Wing Chun. Ng Mui was one of the five elders of the Shaolin Temple but she wasn't always a nun. Her father was one of the eight generals that helped Yeung Jung Wang to ascend to the throne. Yeung Jung Wang was the first emperor of the Ching Dynasty.

After he became emperor, Yeung Jung Wang had his own father and his eight generals killed to reduce the threat to his own power.
Ng Mui was known as Loi Sai Leung at the time. To avenge her father's death, she killed the emperor and went into hiding at the Shaolin Temple where she took the name of Ng Mui.

Already an accomplished martial artist, Ng Mui became the number one skilled elder at the temple. She had studied at the Wudaung Mountain: the birth place of Taoism Temple. Here Ng Mui developed a style of martial arts after observing a snake and crane fighting over a prey for food.

After further research, development, and the observation of a snake and crane, Ng Mui improved the style, which became known as Snake and Crane Eight Fighting techniques. She continued to refine the style further and this style is the predecessor of Wing Chun kung fu.

After fleeing from the Shaolin Temple Ng Mui realised that she would have to save the Shaolin fighting arts from the emperor's efforts to erase all traces of their existence.

Thus, she devised a new, modified system of fighting based on her knowledge of what she had mastered in the temple. In essence, the style utilised techniques of efficiency of motion and direct line attacks and could be perfected in a short period of time.

Ng Mui's best student, a beautiful young girl named Yim Wing Chun, lived with her father, Yim Sam Soak, in a small village where they earned their livelihood by making and selling bean cakes. Yim Wing Chun's popularity in the area and news of her beauty attracted the attention of a local ruffian named Wong.
Although such matters were often customarily prearranged between two families before the birth of the children, and Yim Wing Chun was already promised to Leung Bok Choy, Wong decided he would marry her anyway. Upon presenting himself to ask for her hand in marriage, Wong was flatly rejected by both Yim Wing Chun and her father, so he plotted to take her by force. In a short period of time Ng Mui was able to teach Yim Wing Chun to defend herself. When Wong returned with his men, a confrontation ensued during which Wong was seriously injured by Yim Wing Chun.

Yim Wing Chun continued to study under Ng Mui, and later married Leung Bok Choy. During the years to come, she used the principles of the style that she had learned from Ng Mui and commenced to improve and simplify the art. After refining the art significantly. Yim Wing Chun began to teach it to her husband who was already rather adept in other styles of martial arts. Impressed by Yim Wing Chun's knowledge and ability, he studied her style diligently after the death of Yim Wing Chun he named the art he learned from his wife Wing Chun or "beautiful spring time".

Leung Bok Choy taught the style to Leung Lan Quai who in turn passed the art to Leung Jan who later passed the art to Wing Wah Bo.

Wing Wah Bo taught both Leung Bik and Chan Wah Soon and they both taught Yip Man.

From them the art was passed to my Master Lee Shing who brought the art to the west in the 1960s and settled in London. He started teaching Wing Chun in London Chinatown at the Canton Restaurant which is regarded as the birth place of Wing Chun in the west, and because of fate, I was honoured to have learned from him and carry on this great tradition.

Canton Restaurant
Birthplace of Wing Chun in the West 1960

GULAO WING CHUN

Gulao Wing Chun originates from the village where Dr. Leung Jan retired after leaving Fatshan. Gulao was his home (a small village in Hessian province). Traditionally in Chinese culture the leading Kung Fu master of the village would teach the village youngsters in order that they would be able to protect their village from bandits and raiders who were prevalent at this time and would prey on the weaker villages.

Like all styles of Kung Fu this teaching had two purposes, one was to provide a practical fighting system that would allow the youngsters to defend themselves and their loved ones. The second was to promote health in mind and body to allow the youngsters to live long lives. In addition to the ability to deal out deadly techniques, there had to be some responsibility so the Master must teach the youngsters to be mature, responsible people.

Leung Jan therefore taught a method of Wing Chun that was different from the stylized approach he had previously taught in Fatshan. It was quick and easy to pick up being made up of separate techniques (San Sao) that the beginner could repeat in order to strengthen his body and use very quickly in a fighting situation. Yet there was a lot more to Leung Jan's teaching than mere body movements.

At a more advanced stage the student would realize that these techniques actually encompassed all the underlying principles that make up Wing Chun. Once this was realized the student would be able to apply them with ease to any situation - including fighting with sticks, pole and knife.

Many people today fail to realize that Wing Chun is primarily a set of fighting principles. The basic movements taught are merely a vessel to focus these principles. Today many instructors teach like this, the move must be done this way, rather than focusing on the principle behind the move.

This will allow the student to learn much faster, and allow Wing Chun to become a part of themselves rather than a set of foreign movements that a student must repeat with the hope that they may one day assimilate them. What then happened to this Gulao Wing Chun, and what does it have to do with the man who brought Wing Chun to England? Indeed, who was the man who brought Wing Chun to England?

My Master, Lee Shing, brought Wing Chun to England towards the end of the 1950s. Whose first teacher was Fong Yee Ming, who himself had learnt from Wong Wah Bo who had learnt from Leung Jan. Lee Shing had a real interest in Wing Chun and was a keen disciple who was interested immediately in researching all the different styles of Wing Chun inspired by his knowledge of Gulao Wing Chun.

Lee Shing eventually moved to Hong Kong where he met and trained with Lok Yiu before being introduced to Yip Man in the 50's before being allowed to open up a school on Hong Kong Island - with the opening ceremony being conducted by Grandmaster Yip Man. He then went on to learn from the famous Kung Fu master Ng Jung So, and later Jiu Wan. Even though the present of Wing Chun is more important than the past, it is important to know where your roots lie.

This can give you an insight into the reason behind your art and the techniques used.

The Form consists of the following 12 Handsets:

- Sil Lim Tao
- Dai Lim Tao
- Sam Jheen Choi (Three finger jab)
- Biu Choi (Charging/Thrusting punch)
- Sap Jee Choi (Reverse meridian/Cross hand punch)
- Dip Cheung (Double Butterfly Palm).
Alternating low palm strikes.
- Lan Kiu (Bar Arm Bridge)
- Teet Jee Chiam Kiu (Iron Finger Sinking bridge).
Back fist flowing into low strike followed by low palm strike.

- Tang Ma Bil Chee
 (Rising thrusting finger with phoenix eye)

- Hok Bong (Crane bong).
Level Bong Sau, moving into side body with simultaneous attack

- Wan Wan Yeu (Life after Death).
Using the waist to lean back to
avoid strikes detected late, then using the return
waist power in the hand strike

- Fook Fu (Subduing the Tiger). Mixture between Gan and Fak Sau with phoenix eye.

Also included in the syllabus are:
- Dai Bong (Low soft Bong)
- Fu Mei (low strike to the groin)

- Gwai Lung Na (double Lop Sau)
- Sam Bai Fut (Three bow to Buddha)
- Sam Jhin Chiu (Three arrow blow)
- Fan Kup Choi (uppercut)
- Lien Wan Fai Jeung (linked fast palms)

The important principles like the double bridge - double, Flicking Tan Sau with forward energy to bridge the gap in Chiam Kiu. Gulao Wing Chun teaches you also how to modify these points depending on the situation and how to combine them effortlessly in free flowing techniques so that they are not static but flow freely along with correct footwork.

Saam Dim Boon Kwun (Three-and-a-Half Point Pole) is the standard pole set of the Gulao Wing Chun Kuen system. This version originates from the Lee Shing teachings of Fong Yee-Ming and Fung Sang.

Huen (Circle)
Dim (Point)
Gwot (Cut)
Doy (Pull Back)
Bil (Thrust)

Wu Tip Dao (Shaolin Double Knives) is a double broadsword set of the Gulao Wing Chun Kuen system, This version originates from the Lee Shing teachings of Fong Yee-Ming and Fung Sang. There are many masters denied the existence of Gulao Wing Chun as it is not taught to the public openly. It was until 1980 I was authorised by my master to perform to the public for the first time ever.

Gulao Wing Chun (Dai Lim Tao)
First Public Demonstration July 10th 1980

WING CHUN FAMILY TREE

Ng Mui
|
Yim Wing Chun
|
Leung Bok Choy
|
Leung Lan Quai
|
Leung Jan
|
Wong Wah Bo
/ \
Leung Bik   Chan Wah Shun
|
Yip Man
|
Lee Shing
|
Austin Goh

CHAPTER 4

Training with my master

Conversation with my master

TRAINING WITH MY MASTER

July the 8th 1972 was my first day of training, I remember the first day with him, it was an intense feeling as I was worried that he wouldn't like me as I am not from Hong Kong and so perhaps not going to be fully accepted as his disciple.

But my worry was not for long. He treated me with kindness, looking after me, offering food to me often during training knowing that I was a poor student at that time.

He taught me the finer points of Wing Chun kung fu with great details and explanation. It was amazing. I felt so lucky and privileged to study under him, not knowing then that he was part of a great legacy and history in the Martial Arts world and now I am honured to be part of it, too.

As I used to study in the afternoon and go training and teaching from 6 to 8 pm, then work as a bouncer from 10pm to 3am, I spent most of that period of my life training with him after 4 to 7am in the restaurant - as he also worked until that time, it was a match made in heaven.

My master was a perfectionist; he always said, "why learn so many styles and you can't even perfect one", with this in mind I always practised any new technique he taught me over and over again.

I used to spend hours just practising my techniques, taking my time, practising it over and over again until my master approved of it. It was hard but I loved it - it must be in my blood, for there were other students training there too but most couldn't last more than a few months, as my master wanted to make sure they perfected their techniques before he would show us any other techniques.

Many found it too hard or too long, wanting to master everything as quickly as possible but it was not to be. As I loved to do a lot of kicking in those days (I always wanted to be a top stuntman in movies; it was one of my dreams) and seeing that I was always doing my splits and jumping around he taught me the kicking form technique.

I was so excited practising in my master's house! In the front room I jumped up in the air and tried to kick the ceiling. I tried a few times and failed but being stubborn as usual, I took a deep breath using my chi and one last effort - this time I did it but on the way I smashed the ceiling lamp.

Hearing a loud noise my master and his wife rushed into the room and seeing what happened, my Master's wife (Simo) was flabbergasted and she tried to ban me from ever training in the house. My master just laughed and he even praised my kicking ability. I was so happy and proud of my achievement - sounds crazy, I must be mad.

Training with my master could be tough sometimes. I used to go to his home to train but many times he was not there and sometimes I just waited for hours in the rain and snow for him to come home.

Even when he was at home I would just do my training by myself for hours and once in a while he would correct me and then I would always feel contented.

There were times I was there when he would just ignore me altogether. It could be frustrating and I was not sure where I stood with him. Thinking back maybe he was just trying to test my patience and loyalty.

Nevertheless I preservered and just accepted it while most of his other students were complaining and some just left. Nowadays students are lucky, they pay and come and train. They have it easy and want everything right now. My advice is that no one can achieve it in a short time, you must learn to be patient.

One of the moments that completely changed my way of thinking with my training was when my Master just used a basic tan sau and punching technique to overcome me. Whatever I threw at him - I tried kicking and punching and was trying to grab him but each time he just blocked and punched me and with such ease.

I was very frustrated. Never in a million years would I haved tried and defeat him as I loved and respected him, but I was just trying to use all the different ways to surprise him at least, including things that I had learned before with my uncle. But however hard I tried, I was easily defeated by him. He was laughing and in my mind I thought he must be thinking that I may be young and strong physically, but you couldn't mess with him. After that we went for tea as we usually did after training as most of it was a one-on-one basis. Thinking back I was blessed.

This particular time I asked him how he could block all of my attacking techniques with just one technique. He just smiled and said that training martial arts is a tradition whether it is kung fu, karate or Thai boxing and some people misunderstand and think they have to learn everything under the sun to be good at it whereas you have to know your own style and learn from true masters. Chinese philosophy and thinking might translate to English, but if misunderstood the person will not know that martial arts is both the practice and the philosophy together and therefore may misinterpret the true meaning of the art.

To embark on a journey of martial arts for the Chinese culture is a way of life. The student follows his Master to his death, mainly because no-one can learn and understand one system in just a couple of years - not only will the body not be able to take it but the brain will not be able to absorb all the information. If they try, then it's likely that they will become sick physically and mentally. Wing Chun is an art that has been passed on from generation to generation and only a few selected ones are allowed to carry on this tradition, even if our way of life changes in the future, we still need this basic understanding of respecting your master, others and the art.

I asked my Master again how he managed to defeat me with just one technique. He asked me to remember the time when I had a problem while working in the night club and I was trying to hit this massive guy and could not do it, he still stood there - luckily my friend came and helped me. I recalled I had gone to my Master for advice and he told me to move away from him and give him a side kick to his knee, which I did, and it had worked.

Basically, in martial arts if you just want to learn to defend yourself then the fewer techniques you learn, the better. If you have too many techniques then you can become confused and in a real situation you could panic and freeze and all your training goes out of the window. Defending yourself in real fighting is nothing like fighting in the gym where you know everything is in a controlled environment and fight scenes in films are carefully choreographed so it looks good for the audience to enjoy. In real life it is so different, your life is in danger and you could be injured or killed, you just don't know, therefore you need to practise one or two techniques for blocking and striking to perfection, then you will have a good chance to defeat your adversary.

Our conversation continued and I asked him what techniques would be best for me, he said that each and every person is individual depending on their build, whether big or small, for speed training you must let your internal power lead you.

I asked him again how I could achieve this. He said that I needed to learn to relax and breathe properly first, then practise chain punching in a relaxed way. I mentioned that I already was doing this for a few hours every day, and he replied that after five years I might achieve it.

I was taken aback why so long, I asked him straight away, he replied that the human race are the same now as they were a thousand years ago, wanting everything instantly whereas your body and mind takes time to cultivate and your mind also needs time to absorb all the information — something you cannot hurry, like nature, everything grows and bloom when the season is right.

I nodded with approval and yet wanted to know more. I wondered if there was a grabbing and kicking technique in Wing Chun. He told me that of course there was - but for my physical build, striking would be better and the techniques that I needed to learn and practise were the "breaking power of grabbing".

If I used my then current grabbing technique against bigger guys I would have certainly lost in a fight. The only way I could overcome my disadvantage was to learn and practise striking and grabbing with speed and power. I nodded with understanding.

He continued by saying that if I just wanted to learn to defend myself then perfecting a few techniques is more than enough but if I wanted to study martial arts as an art, to be a master; then it would be a life long journey. While I love all my physical training and fighting I also understood that one day I would also be old, so hopefully my martial arts skill, knowledge and philosophy would benefit me in my old age.

I thanked him and I cherished all our tea time conversations, it was so valuable to me to understand, not just training, but how to interact with other humans the way my Master did - it was just simply awesome. I realise that martial arts training is not just punching and kicking trying to prove who can beat each other but it is much deeper and that changed my way of thinking. Through my Master's great teaching I was starting to mature.

A CONVERSATION WITH MY MASTER

My master was a very private person. One evening during our usual tea time he looked very sad; I could see it in his eyes. He told me that life for him was also tough before coming to London. The problem for him was not being able to speak English and not knowing what to do after losing everything: his business and his home in China.

During the Cultural Revolution he had to flee from China without his wife, son or daughter. He decided to come to England to seek his fortune and a better life for all of them. It was really tough for him as he had to leave his family behind and on his own took a journey aboard a ship to the west not knowing anything what lay ahead. The ship took months to arrive in Liverpool.

He was heartbroken leaving his family behind. His aim was to arrive in England first, then hopefully save enough money for the passage to bring his family over. It took him a few years of hard graft before he saved enough money to bring his family over. I was touched by this man's determination to seek a better life for his family and his willingness to sacrifice everything for them. He said that upon arriving in Chinatown, London he too had to find odd jobs to survive and it was worse than in Hong Kong, but instead of dwelling on what he was doing he just got on with it, thinking of his family which gave him the determination to save enough money for their passage here. Eventually he did it and felt so much happier when they arrived and could be a family again.

I was always moaning to him about facing all sorts of problems while in London, yet my problems were trivial compared to his. I had never seen the soft side of him, before it had always been about martial arts.

It was then when I realised how selfish I had been, wanting to learn everything from him, without truly knowing him, without understanding that this man had suffered a lot in the past, but graciously, suffered in silence. I realised and understood that sometimes he too needed to show emotions, he too could feel down. He was also human.

This was an incredible story and similar to my grandfather's, and many other older Chinese people, abroad in the west in those days. I heard similar stories repeated over and over again when I met many old masters in America. I still remember one grand master of 101 years old in Los Angeles who told me his life story. He was very fond of me because I listened and respected him as my elder. It is probably the Chinese culture that reinforces that one must learn to respect and listen to one's elders.

He told me when he left China he was promised by some people that he could have work in a restaurant in Chinatown but upon arriving he was instead sent to work in the railway industry, blowing up mines with dynamite to open up routes for the railway track to be laid.

It was a life threatening job particularly as it was always the Chinese who had to go and light the fuse of the dynamite before quickly running away, as far as they could before it exploded.

Sometimes they tripped or fell and couldn't get far enough away from the explosion and got maimed or killed. In those days Chinese women were not allowed to come to America and it was a hard time for most migrants because if you wanted to bring your family over you must have enough money to bribe the officials and even their own fellow Chinese.

The experiences of these people and the work they did fascinated me and made me proud to be Chinese - yet thinking deeper; with 5000 years of great civilisation how come a great country's people came to be like this where its citizens were being punished for trying to live their dreams after having no choice but to flee their homeland.

The wisdom and their experiences are so different yet they can be the same, each wanting to better their lives for themselves and their families. The struggles and obstacles they faced along the way, their drive, and how they dealt with it really fascinated me, the human mind and spirit is by far greater than all.

These people just got on with it and dealt with the problems without complaining or feeling sorry for themselves. This reminded me that just because I was a tough guy and could fight my way out of a situation; it does not make me a real man, all the macho stuff has no meaning against all these great human experiences I had heard about - I had finally started to grow up.

Life is not just about just oneself, thinking how to take advantage of others for selfish benefits. It is about giving, trying and doing. With this conversation I became closer to my Master - he was not just my teacher but he was also someone who inspired me. In my heart I felt a sense of belonging, like I had found a long lost family - it made me so happy.

MY MASTER'S STUDENTS

Students who trained with my master were all Chinese from Hong Kong. What I did not understand as a fellow Chinese was being subjected to prejudice by them yet they told my Master I was not pure Chinese and did not deserve to be taught by him. Luckily my Master did not listen to them.

Some of his so-called students still denied the fact that I now had become my Master's rightful successor, which I had not expected but it was meant to be. I had proven to him my martial arts spirit, character and loyalty all these years, teaching and spreading his art to the world, which none of his students managed to do.

Even though I faced jealousy, envy and prejudice from all these so-called kung fu brothers of mine during my training - I just got on with it and there were two of his students that always stood by me and encouraged me and for that I am grateful.

I had to promise to my Master not to reveal the kicking form Gulao Wing Chun and Human Energy training to others until after his death. I kept my promise to him.

Maybe it was the way my parents brought me up to respect and honour and always remember the people who had helped me along the way. Without this help I would had given up when faced with these situations during my training with my master. Yet whenever my master needed help I was the only one there and none of them would show up.

I remember there was a man who claimed that he was the direct disciple of Yip Man and told people that my Master's Wing Chun was not in the same family and wanted to challenge my master, none of his student's dared take up the challenge, but to me it was just another sparring session so I took him on in front of my master and his students. He was good and I must say he knew his stuff and managed to punch me on my cheek.

I took it and staggered back, he took advantage of the situation and charged in to knock me down. My vision was blurred and I could barely see. As he approach I jumped to the side and kicked him in the rib cage. He fell like a log and went unconscious. We called the ambulance and his ribs were broken - luckily he survived. After this incident some of my master's students accused me of ruining the Wing Chun image by using a Tae Kwon Do kick to defeat the guy, disgracing the family.

I asked my master what is wrong with these people? If they are that good why don't they take the challenge, yet only I would. He told me that I did a good job and that guy was one of the top Wing Chun fighters in Hong Kong - but he only knew the straight line Wing Chun not Gulao or the kicking techniques that I was taught. These arts are not meant to be taught openly only closed door disciples can learn these techniques. He told me to ignore all these people and keep up with my training.

After this I would take over my Master's class whenever he was not there and as my reputation grew I travelled all over to show my skills, knowledge and my master's teaching to the world. It was hard work connecting with different cultures. They embraced my teaching, making me feeling very satisfied. However nowadays people create a website and write whatever they want to attract students and argue over one another on the Internet, calling themselves masters and grandmasters. It's a crazy world.

It makes me think - where is the martial arts spirits giving themselves titles like candy. What can I do? I lost tens years without understanding all about the Internet and how to go about attracting students from it. Now I am starting to understand and it is not too late, I still believe that my past experience, knowledge, skills and wisdom will help me to send my message across. This is the new world of technology that I need to and will embrace.

For every new challenge one must start with the first step.

CHAPTER 5

Personal Training
Student to Master Level

MY PERSONAL TRAINING

Part of my training was to increase my muscle power by going to the gym and doing weight training. I built up quite a bit of muscle but was horrified to find out that during my sparring session I had slowed down considerably.

I went to my master to seek his advice. His advice was that I must learn to relax the muscles again after my weight training by practising the 3 vibrating hands technique to loosen them, followed by relaxed chain punching; by practising this I would still maintain my speed and power.

In order to toughen my arms I practised on the wooden dummy. But after a while the arms and the legs of the dummy broke and it was hard to replace so I decided to ask someone to replace the wooden arms and legs with metal.

SHINBONE CONDITIONING

To condition my shinbone I practised kicking on trees and a wooden pole wrapped with thick ropes, then my master would massage my shin with his chi energy to reduce the bruises and any internal injuries. After that I had to roll a milk bottle on the shin bones to strengthen them further. I have to say it was very painful at first but once I got used to it, it was ok.

In Wing Chun training, a student first learns the form Sil Lim Tao.

This gives you a clear understanding of this unique fighting system, by practising it you will learn to protect your centre line and also to balance your energy within yourself. You must also practise in a relaxed way so that the chi can flow to every part of your body thus strengthening you. It took me 3 years to perfect, only then my Sifu would continue teaching me the advanced techniques.

He would always remind me what is the point of learning further while your foundation is not established properly? Even though I had trained in Malaysia in the past I was all over the place in my stance and techniques and if I wanted to be a true master of Wing Chun then I must start from the basics and I must make sure my foundation is solid before I move on to bigger things.

With that in mind I always practise my Sil Lim Tao everyday until now.

FINGER PRESSUPS

In order to toughen my arms I chose a tree with a strong trunk in my master's garden and hit my arms on it everyday then after 3 years I was ready for my iron arms training to strengthen my bones further.

My master told me to find five iron rods about two feet long and three inches widde, bind them together. I practised my back fist on it everyday by hitting it with the arms repeatedly an hour everyday for three years - it was hard. Both my arms were bruised, black and blue and it was tough training, but I just wanted to succeed. With this training I was able to break bricks and hard object with ease. I remember one day one master who trained in Shaolin kung fu iron hand technique told me that Wing Chun structure based on Centre line fighting is easily defeated if he swing his arm from the side to me and will be able to knock me out - in other words I will not be able to block it. I told him the only way to find out is to put his theory to the test against me.

He agreed and came in strong with a hook punch to the side of my face, I stood strong extend my hands out in a blocking position (fat sau) and blocked it while his whole centre line was open and therefore he walked right into my punch.

His nose was bleeding badly and his arm was broken too. A cry of agony echoed into the room and I took him to the hospital .

After 6 months I went to visit him at his home. Apparently his arm and nose were both damaged so badly by my block and punch. I apologised to him saying that I did not mean to do that but as the result of him coming in so strong, the impact on my arm and punch did the damage. He did not say anything but I left him 500 pounds to help him out as he could not work for at least 6 months.

Thinking of it, I must have improved in my training and I was feeling very contented with my progress.

STUDENT TO MASTER LEVEL

The year was 1978, it was a great day for me, my Sifu took me aside and told me it was time for me to receive my "Sifu Jai" literally "Small Sifu" level or translated, instructor level that would eventually lead me to master level. I was only 24 years old; I asked him am I ready? He said that he had not met a student like me who totally respected him and followed his teaching without any questions asked and I would be able to spread the art of Wing Chun for him. When he said that I felt so happy and very emotional too. I was away from my home and family and yet he took me under his wing, taught me his kung fu and treated me like his son. I was so grateful and lucky.

But I still had to pass a few tests laid down by him... I needed to prove my upper physical body strength by doing 1000 press ups, followed by 800 kicks based on the Wing Chun 8 kicks. I also had to show him my Wing Chun knowledge - my Wooden dummy form, pole form, butterfly knives form, Chi Sau and sparring with some of my kung fu brothers. Lastly I had to do close contact sparring (Chi Sau) with my master; It was intense; I felt like I had lost 20 pounds! I was sweating and feeling the pressure, it took 5 hours.

During the Chi Sau with my Sifu - I realised he was different, much faster and so precise in his techniques. It was eye opening for me. He told me being a master in Wing Chun is not just practising punching and kicking; the body, mind and soul must be connected, to generate explosive power in one punch and kick. I was totally exhausted physically and mentally. What an experience!

No one ever grows great until he is focused, dedicated and disciplined.

Swearing Ceremony Receiving
Sifu Level Certification 1978

Certificate awarded to me by
my Master after my grading 1978

CHAPTER 6

Opening Wing Chun School

The Art of Breaking

OPENING THE FIRST WING CHUN SCHOOL IN LONDON'S CHINATOWN

In 1973 I opened the first Wing Chun school in Europe accepting students from all different cultures and races, which was unheard of at that time. I later moved the kwoon (school) to Covent Garden and took a 3000 square foot space to have my first full time training centre and as far as I know it was the largest and only full time Wing Chun centre not only in England but also in Europe.

I put together a grading system for my students which was a new idea and drew criticism from some circles. Uniform and different colour sashes were introduced too. Chi kung was taught along with full contact fighting. Nowadays most of the Wing Chun schools have followed this system, which is very flattering to see. At least my influence in this art can be seen in most of these schools all over the world and this makes me happy.

Kicking, Wooden Dummy and Wing Chun Knives form were taught openly without any secret. I designed fingerless gloves for free sparring long before mixed martial arts.

I also designed a special ring made from rattan, similar to one I used to practise with when I was 10 years old and found very helpful in perfecting my techniques. This helps students to practise their Chi Sau (the art of closed contact fighting). By practising with it regularly students will be able to perfect their techniques to a higher level. I named it the "Chi Sau Ring".

I always believe that if an art is not taught openly and correctly it will eventually die.

In 1974 after the death of Grandmaster Yip Man I was authorized by the Yip Man Martial Arts Association in Hong Kong to be their official representative of Wing Chun in Europe.

My master later promoted me to Master Advanced Level and an official certificate personally signed by him in 1978 was presented to me. It was great honour for me and I thank him for his teaching and choosing me to be his rightful representative.

What a day - I can never forget it. It was the happiest time of my life.

I also produced the first Wing Chun videos in 1982 showing the complete Wing Chun system.

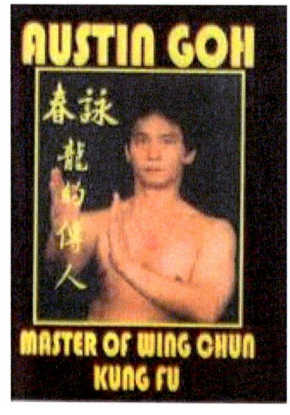

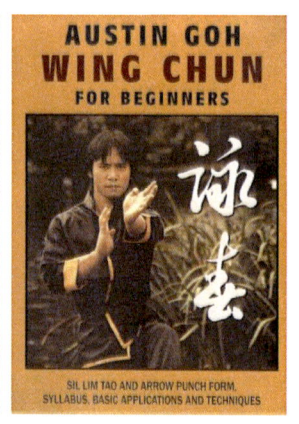

Below is the curriculum of forms taught by me. These include Wing Chun's three main forms as well as the extended curriculum which includes Gulao forms. The color of the sash indicates the level at which the form is learned by a student.

Yellow Sash:

Sil Lim Tao (Little Idea)
Jin Kuen (Arrow Punch)

Green Sash:

Chiam Kiu (Seeking the Bridge)
Sar Bao Kuen (Sandbag Form)

Blue Sash:

Sup Luk Gerk Faat (Kicking Techniques)

Red Sash:

Chi kung Breathing Form Bil Chee (Thrusting Fingers)

Brown

Pole Form

Black:

Muk Yang Jong (Wooden Dummy)
Ng Mui Sil Lim Tao (Female Little Idea)
Inch Punch Form

THE ART OF BREAKING

Wing Chun kung fu was never into breaking bricks but I defied this tradition and I went to demonstrate breaking concrete blocks, bricks and pavement slabs in my shows. Most of these kung fu masters were so horrified to see this because they said that I was practising karate and destroying the good name of kung fu.

They argued that Chinese martial arts does not include breaking. However I raised the point that how can one show the power of Wing Chun if one does not show it through breaking ability.

If you do not possess that how can you expect to knock out an opponent. Chinese martial arts is based on skill, techniques and deep philosophy and then power and strength. It's not just jumping up and down doing complicated moves and somersaulting with a pole or sword

They must understand that people in the west are more realistic and that they only want to see real action - they cannot see the deep philosophy and inner strength of Wing Chun until they had been training for a long time in the art. In the mean time I needed to attract new students and I needed to adapt in society, rather than just practising forms and set patterns - which is ok from the beginning but they needed to learn power training, sparring and conditioning. It is like learning to swim without going in the water. It is not realistic and to me it's cheating the student.

But these few older Chinese masters from different styles did not agree and wanted to stop me from teaching my art. They complained to my master and a meeting was set up to clarify this. I sought my master for advice asking him if I was wrong. He said that all these people are jealous in a similar way to what they did to Bruce Lee in the States, I did the right thing; Chinese martial arts is expressing oneself, not just a fixed pattern learning form after form and thinking that they can defend themselves.

He told me that these so called master are just students claiming to be masters and I should just ignore them and get on with it.

I asked him what about the meeting? He told me that we should go, be respectful but they will not do anything to me because they were not trained to the same level. He mentioned that they were just amateurs and not professionals and even though he did not say much to me about my progress, that he could see the way I trained with my heart and soul not worrying about getting hit. He told me "The effort you put in is tremendous" - he had yet to witness a similar student and that is what he wanted in a disciple.

We went to the meeting and they accused me that I had no respect for Chinese culture and that I was not even Chinese as I came from Malaysia not from Hong Kong! They made it clear that ther taughtI should not be teaching kung fu in that way.

I told them that they were amateurs, either cooks or restaurant owners and that this is not professional enough - they should mind their own business and leave me alone. Time had changed and this was the new world now and a new generation. All these traditions are good but we need to learn to adapt in the new society, no doubt I was born in Malaysia my grandparents are as Chinese as any of them so what is the problem? They were angry with me asking my master how could he let me behave like this? My master told them that I was a big boy now and he couldn't keep telling me what I should do. He told them that I was the first Chinese master in Europe to teach like this and he said "we should support him and this will make us Chinese, proud in England".

They disagreed at first, eventually I told them the only way now is to have a duel. One master said that if he hit me once I would be dead in three days time. I replied that as they were my elders I would let any one of them hit and kick me once, but in return I would punch or kick them once and whoever it was - would die on the spot.

None of them dared to accept my challenge and looked sheepish. My master saw this and told them "we are all getting old now, why do we need to interfere with the next generation, they have their way. Whether it is good or bad; we need to support him and we should not be stubborn like this".

Finally they left without saying anything but in my heart I felt that you cannot please everyone. I thanked my master for his support and carried on with the way I was teaching until now.

CHAPTER 7

My view on training in modern Martial Arts

Training in the Art

Achieving Sifu Level

MY VIEW ON TRAINING IN MODERN MARTIAL ARTS

Training in martial arts depends on the individual. Some like to do it for health, some for self defence and others like to do it for a living and turn professional like Thai boxers, Mix martial artists and boxers. Only a handful like me practise it as a lifestyle.

Martial arts are divided into all these categories.

So that everyone can enjoy it in a different way. If you choose the one that you like then follow it and try to enjoy the training.

If you want to train martial arts as a lifestyle then obviously the training is different from going for competitions and just fighting. It's a life long journey and it involves years of dedication. training and harnessing the art to perfection.

Learning from your master, it is not to be used for fighting it is the way to find inner peace within yourself, your journey on earth. Connecting your body mind and soul for self cultivation in harmony within yourself and nature that is the true spirit of a martial art student final goal.

If you are training in martial arts for competitions then the training is completely different. You need to toughen your body, increase your stamina and practise techniques like grabbing, punching and throwing while in the cage as it is in mix martial arts fighting.

You also need to get used to the competition atmosphere by having lots of pre-tournaments fights to prepare yourself for your opponents.

For those want to practise martial art,for health then human energy level one training programme is more than enough for you to practise and maintain a long and healthy life.

It is not the art, it is the person who does the art whether they have been taught properly and have spent the time, dedication and patience to achieve a high level.

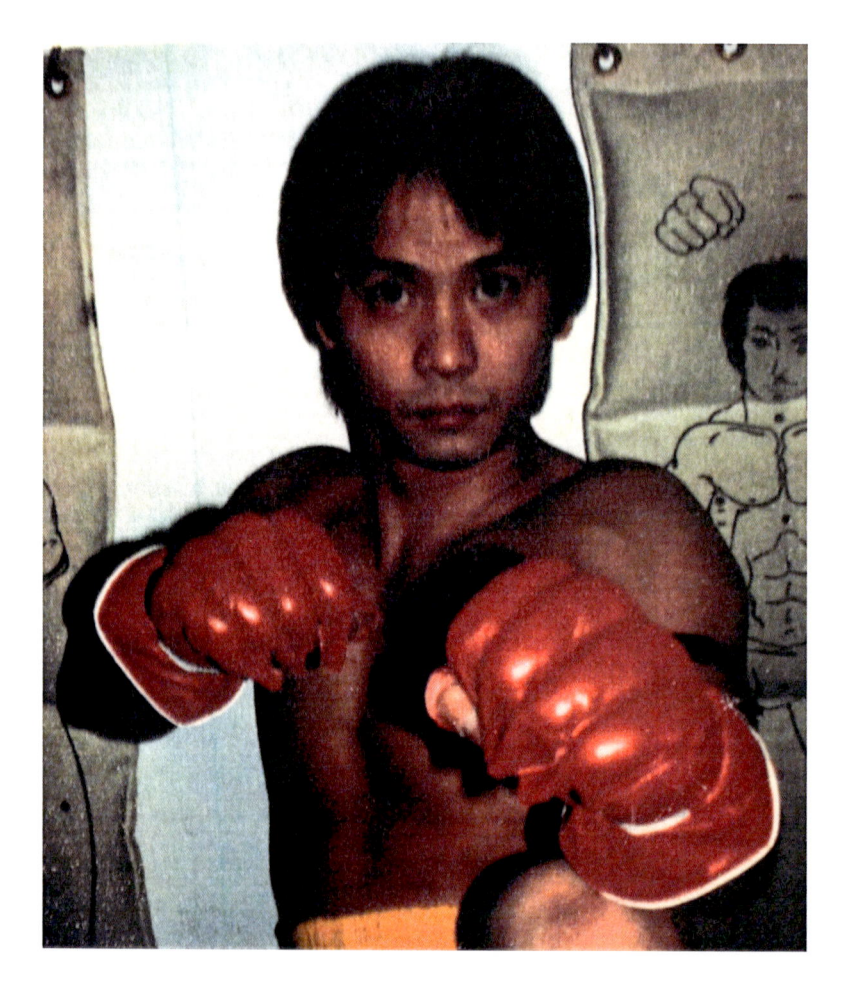

MY FIGHTING DAYS

TRAINING IN THE ART

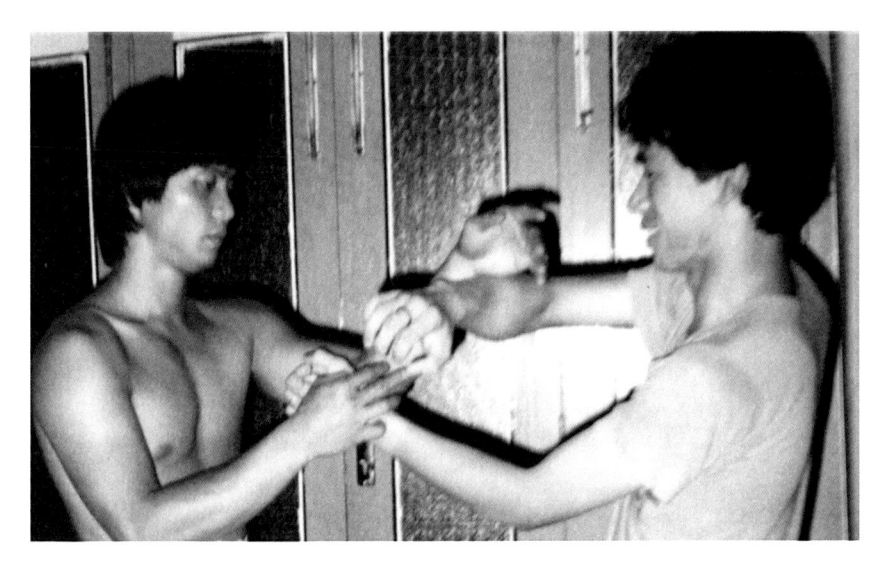

My advice to Wing Chun students is to learn to relax your body from top to bottom so that the chi can flow easily. Thus strengthening your internal organs, first this will improve your power greatly in the future.

It is important not to rush into the training, make sure you master the foundation before you can move on to the more advanced techniques. A student must practise their breathing technique properly and correctly. Do not just practise your hand techniques like chi sau and hands drill only, you must learn to combine your kicking techniques too.

In free sparring you must learn to control your strength - don't try just to win, you need to try out all the techniques you have learnt, during free fighting training.

I always notice most students just want to win during free sparring, resulting in their techniques worsening. Sparring or free fighting has nothing to do with street fighting - it helps you improve your fighting skill to a higher level.

While practising all the three main forms make sure you learn to breathe properly so that the inner strength can connect with your physical power in order to produce the explosive power to be able to knock any opponent down instantly.

Footwork must also be practised correctly so that it will improve your movement greatly and this will increase your speed during punching and kicking in a sparring or in a real situation.

It is most important to be patient; it is good to know all the techniques and theory but it contributes to just 30 percent of your training, the rest is total dedication in practical training like:

1 . Practising and perfecting the techniques daily

2. Conditioning: toughening your arms legs and body
Physical training like press ups and sit ups.

Flexibility: stretching to loosen up the joints
Stamina training: running and skipping, punching the sand bag, kicking the hanging bag and wooden dummy training

3. Chi kung training to strengthen your organs

I hope you understand now that it is not easy for anyone to train and master an art completely, it does take time, total dedication and guidance from a good master. I advise you to be patient and always try to practise regularly so that you will always keep in touch with the art, making you stronger and better in the future.

May I wish you good luck in your quest for martial arts perfection.

ACHIEVING SIFU LEVEL

Mastering any form of martial arts requires hard work and total dedication. As we live in the modern world, most people will not have time to commit themselves fully to train in an art, especially Wing Chun, properly.

Nevertheless we can still practise it to a high standard if we take our time training in this system.
In order to practise Wing Chun properly, a student must first find a true master; it can be difficult nowadays, as so many claim to be original, traditional, or proper masters teaching the art. I have set out rules for all my students who wish to be a master in the art.

Firstly they must have passed through my grading programme to receive their Instructor first degree - normally 3 to 5 years, after that they will be taught how to be a good instructor for another year, then depending on their effort and dedication, I will recommend them to go for instructor level 2 black sash.

Once they have achieved that, they will be allowed to open their own training school under my name. I believe that if students are not trained properly and correctly under my guidance then how can they spread the art properly?

Students training at weekend courses and abroad in the east for one or two years and then calling themselves Master or Sifu is not accepted in my organisation.

To be considered as a Sifu or Master of Wing Chun one must be at least 50 years of age and should have had 15 years of teaching experience. Then he will be promoted by me to Sifu level.

CHAPTER 8

Challenges in the Kwoon

Closing down a Wing Chun School

CHALLENGES IN THE KWOON

There was one incident when a top master in kicking kept going on about how bad Wing Chun was - "it's just a dance" - bragging that he knocked down a top 55 years old master with just one kick. In my mind was what sort of a martial arts master beats up an older man?

Knowing this I told him to come to my kwoon, and have a go at me. I was also hard headed, I let him kick me on my body and even my head, I took everything he threw at me and said to him "is a kung fu master that soft that he can't take punishment?", then I said "now it's my turn to knock you out with one punch" and without any delay the next kick he threw at me I blocked and punched him on his nose with such speed and power he staggered back and was bleeding badly but still wanted to continue as his pride and ego was hurt.
I said "being Chinese no matter where you're from, we don't destroy each other. It's a disgrace." - I warned him if he tried to kick me again, this time I would break his leg and that was the chance he would have to take. Hearing this his students led him away and I never saw him again.

There were others but they were also sent packing by me. It is not the art that makes the man, it is the man that makes the art. I always tell my students being good in martial arts does not give you a licence in the street.

So always respect others unless they are the ones who want to be nasty to you then you can take action. There were also students who had trained with me and after receiving their black sash came back to challenge me to see whether they too could try to defeat me in sparring; at first I thought how could people behave like this? You teach them and they turn against you. Is this a normal behaviour in the West? Or it is a different culture and normal thinking that a student thinks once they have their black sash, if they can defeat their master in a sparring match, they think that they have overtaken him in the skill of martial arts. This is not tennis or swimming. The words "martial arts" are often misunderstood. Martial is to do with fighting, arts means skill and knowledge passed on from master to student. However in Chinese culture, kung fu means a skill attained from hard work, discipline and respect both to the one who teaches you, and to others.

How can a son try to physically beat up his own father? Is that a civilised way of thinking or is it a free society where everyone is equal? To me that is confusing and does not make sense. I can understand that we live in a commercial and fast society and everyone wants to be better than each other, so why not challenge people from different styles and prove to them how good you are after training with your master like the way I did. I was shocked and hurt at first. Many years a go I looked after one of my instructors since he was 16 years old. He came from a violent family background and was constantly beaten by his father.

I took him in, opened up my heart and let him stay in my gym giving him good shelter and taught him for free- once he got his black sash after ten years with me, he turned against me by saying I was too slow, or even criticised my Wing Chun skills, as he said that people nowadays are into kick boxing and mixed martial arts.

He said my way of thinking and training methods were far too old fashioned and out of date. I told him to put on his gloves and show me how great his mixed martial arts were, in my heart I thought "should I go for it and knock him down?, or just give him a chance to just teach him a lesson?". He went for it, kicking and punching with the intention of knocking me down, trying to defeat me but was frustrated- I blocked him with ease. He was getting extremely frustrated that he could not do anything to knock me down. Eventually I told him enough is enough.

He should have apologised to me, if he wasn't going to I wanted him out of my gym. It hurt my heart when I thought that I had treated him like my own, just like the way my master had treated me. As I turned around to walk away I felt him running toward me, when I turned around he punched me on my nose so hard that I staggered backwards.

I was blinded for a second as the tears from my eyes were making my vision blurred - in fact I was blind at that moment but I could sense that a strong kick was coming towards my face- in an instant I turned and sent my chi to my arms not just to block it, but to break his shin bones. He fell to the floor holding his leg and screaming. One of my students had to call an ambulance to take him to the hospital.

After 5 months I received a lawsuit from him as he had legal aid accusing me that I was aggressive and violent to him and I broke his leg on purpose. He wanted £50,000 compensation. We went to court but because there were witnesses who had seen what had happened he had no case to answer.

That took nearly 3 years to resolve. I was worried and saddened to go through this with someone I had trusted and taught, who had turned against me. Ever since then if anyone wanted to challenge me I would ask them to sign an agreement so that they would not sue me. There were two who did sign it as they wanted to prove a point to me, that time I didn't waste any time with my speed and power, they were knocked out cold in less than a second not knowing what hit them.

Wing Chun is not a sport, it is an ancient skill passed on from master to student, one learns to respect and discipline oneself, it is an art, not two people trying to kill each other in a cage. If they want to go that way, it is their choice but show respect to the one who taught you. Since then no-one has dared to come to my kwoon to challenge me because in the real fight the master will show no mercy.

Not many people in the martial arts world understand true respect. If you play with fire prepare to get burned; as Confucius said "what you do not want done to yourself, do not do to others." In other words if you want to hit someone you too must be prepared to get hit, if you're not, then don't do it. That is why in any fighting situation I always prepare my body and mind for all sorts of nasty situations.
My master always said in Wing Chun thinking there are only two words vertical or horizontal. The one who is standing is always right.

To prove to the people out there that Wing Chun was a tough fighting art. I invited many different masters from different styles to have a sparring session with me. Twelve took up my challenge. I told them to line up and take turn to try to and knock me out - they were given three minutes each. When I looked at them, I observed that there were some tough boys waiting to take me on and wanting to teach me a lesson. I thought to myself "am I out of my mind? can I handle them? If I fail my reputation and my school will be finished". Nevertheless I went through it and knocked out eight of them with my speed and power and none of them saw what hit them. There was blood everywhere on the floor. The rest of the people refused to take part after seeing how brutal and powerful I was. After that no one dared to even come near my kwoon to challenge me.

But most of my students had gone. Rumours out there said I was only there to beat up my students and not to teach them. I felt upset and thought that maybe all I cared about was being a tough guy and that all the martial art spirit was out of the window. Had I gone to the dark side?, what had I become? If I behaved this way my student too would be like this and this is not what training Wing Chun is all about. But after many years of experience, most people are so ignoranct and arrogant you can't talk to them they need to be taught a lesson.

I went to my master and asked him if what I did was wrong. He said people here do not understand how to respect people, especially so called martial artists here. They believe that the art is to use for hurting one another and once they have learned it they call themselves "master" without any authority, what I had done was right in a way but sometime some people might not see it that way.

They think that you are a bully with no culture - but there are some that need to be taught a lesson, if they don't feel the pain inflicted on them then they think that you are weak. How many fights must you have to prove yourself? There is no point teaching someone who does not want to understand what is true martial arts meaning.

I told my students that I am here to teach them and if they think I am not good enough they should go somewhere else. That if they wanted to test me they should accept the consequences. This to me is not respectful and I don't need students who behave in this way. Since then most people seem to behave better towards me. . I wonder why?

CLOSING DOWN A WING CHUN SCHOOL IN LONDON

In those days people who were not qualified to teach Wing Chun were not allowed to open schools freely like nowadays. If they did so without my master's permission I would go and close them down. Before I went I would always prepare my body and mind to deal with any difficulties I might encounter. I always sought advice from my master and would seek permission from him too.

There was a top karate master who claimed to be a Wing Chun master but was teaching karate instead, so I went to his Kwoon with the intention of closing it down. He was a big guy, tough and physically strong like a bull. He knew who I was and started shouting and swearing at me, saying that it was none of my business what he was teaching. I told him he could teach anything he wanted but don't call it Wing Chun; it was our culture that he was ruining.

He told me that Wing Chun was not strong enough- he was adding karate techniques to make it stronger. I just told him to shut up or I would shut him up. He was so angry that he launched at me with his strong punch- he was powerful but so slow, I could see it coming and hit immediately with my speed punch on his nose, followed by chain punching to knock him down.

He was a tough boy and he sure could take some punishment from me but he was knocked out by my chain punching. I left after that, but the next day the police came to our kwoon and charged me with assault and threatening behaviour towards others.

My master bailed me out; I was later given one year's suspended sentence. I asked my master after that incident, how come all his other students just talked a lot and yet did nothing to help and protect his good name, were they afraid or simply not tough enough to deal with all these situations? Why was it only me?

He told me that he had only taught thirty Chinese students and only five completed the center line Wing Chun system. Just two he would consider as his diciples had completed the Gulao Wing Chun too. Me and one of my seniors. Most of his so called students wanted to learn from him just for their own personal gain.

They did not understand what true respect really was, and also being Chinese they feared to lose face if they got beaten, but I told him that in a real situation you must also learn to accept defeat; if not how can you improve, and how can an art progress with time? He was very impressed with me when he heard that. He praised me and taught me some advanced techniques.

I can understand now that when one of his students who was my senior - used my Master's name and kung fu skills to open a gambling den in a basement in Chinatown, attracting all sorts of bad people and declaring himself as the boss of Chinatown, bullying others and collecting protection money from the restaurant, it was bad news for my master, and his reputation in Chinatown was tainted by this.

My Master took me aside and told me the situation and I told him Chinatown is a small place- I have friends from the East end, and I could ask the Maltese and Jamaican boys to sort him out, just let me know.

He told me this had to be sorted out the Chinese way, so I asked him what his intention was.

He told me to go to him and ask him to have a meeting with my master. So I went to send him the message, he was cocky at first but I insisted that if he did not agree, I would deal with him myself and so reluctantly he agreed. During the meeting I had never seen my master raise his voice until then.

My master warned him that if he were to carry on his bad behaviour in Chinatown, I would have to close him down. No doubt he might be my senior, but they knew I was a hard nut to crack, and fearless too. He left and after that we did not hear anymore from him.

Since then I have realised that it's not worth it because people will always abuse the art and in the modern world they have the law to protect them while they are abusing another person's good name. I told my master this is England, the people here did not understand our ways and that we just needed to protect our name and nowadays people are selfish and only care about themselves. They do not understand the true meaning of respect.

LONDON CHINATOWN 1982

RECEIVING THREATS

In the 80's and 90's more and more people started to train in Wing Chun and many self proclaimed masters were opening schools everywhere. It was like opening sweet shops everyday, claiming to be teaching the real stuff and infighting. Becoming a master overnight by a training a few months in Hong Kong or China and coming back with certificates - it was crazy. At that time I received a lots of threats and challenges far more than in the 70s - but they were just words.

There was one guy who claimed to be an ex-army boy and was beating up his students to show how tough he was and kept calling me to challenge me. I told him to come to my place but he did not. After receiving so many abusive phone calls, I could not take it anymore. I decided to take the matter into my own hands and went to him. When he saw me he was surprised and shocked, he swore at me and 4 of his boys surrounded me, I was prepared and I took my nunchaku out and smashed them in their legs and heads seeing that he ran to the street and I chased after him but he ran away.

It was crazy. Later in the evening the police came to arrest me and this time they wanted to charge me with assault with a weapon and also GBH (grievous bodily harm). I knew of that when they came to arrest me in the club where I worked. I hid myself in the big freezer behind the back of the kitchen my friend cover the entrance with rubbish so that they could not find me. It was bloody freezing and I stayed in one corner and meditated. I am not sure how many hours passed but eventually my friend opened the door when the police were gone, it was a relief to see daylight. After that I went into hiding for nearly a year before I dared to set foot back into Chinatown.

Reflecting on this I decided not to get involved in any more challenges. I had done more than enough to keep up the good name of Wing Chun while others just tried to benefit from my success.

The World is never a fair place and it will never be. I began to accept the reality of human behaviour which can be cruel and nasty sometimes. To some people they may think that I might have been childish and immature ; behaving like a hooligan, in life sometimes there are situations where one has no choice but to take action, it is easy for anyone to say this or that but they were not in my situation. How can they comment. What I did was to stand up for my rights to protect my self and my hard earned reputation which took years to achieve and I was brought up to be kind and respectful to others regardless of who and what they were, and will always stand by this principle.

Most of these so called master do not have a clue of the basic principle of martial arts training, let alone teaching others. What I had to go through in learning and teaching sometimes could be heartbreaking - people come and go and there were many times I had to pay the rent of the training school from my own pocket. Luckily I had my shop and other businesses to support it. I did not give up and I still teach to the best of my knowledge whether there is one student a hundred. My passion for martial arts outweighs all of these obstacles and I am sure I will be still teaching improving and learning for a very long time.

CHAPTER 9

Students who trained with me

STUDENTS WHO TRAINED WITH ME

When I first started teaching in Chinatown, London, my students were mostly Chinese. Very few westerners were allowed to join, even though I was teaching openly to the public, deep down I was worried how my Master would react if he found out that I openly taught his art to westerners. Nevertheless, most of the Chinese students were from Hong Kong and mostly were restauranteurs having their own family takeaway buisness. There was one particular student that reminded me of how I was when I was his age, he was 18 at that time and was the only son in the family.

The main reason he started training with me was to learn to protect himself and his family business because they were always subject to abuse, racism and people were trying to collect protection money from them. It was too much for the family to handle as the perpetrators were there most evenings trying to cause trouble.
Even the police were called but once they had gone the perpetrators would come back again making it hard for the family to endure any more. I went to his restaurant and stayed there for a week to help them to deal with these bullies. One evening six of them came along, chanting racist and verbal abuse to the parents, so I went behind them with a stick behind my back and whacked it across the back of their legs - three of them fell to the ground and the rest stood there, stunned by my actions. I held the stick and pointed at them indicating that if they moved I would use it again.

My student leapt over the counter and together we cornered them. They got scared and dragged their friends on the floor away, and I warned them never to come back. I carried on staying there for a few more nights fearing that they might come back with more people but after a week they seemed to have gone for good. I told my student if they came back again, to lock the door and under no circumstances go out in the street to confront them as this was far too dangerous as they might have had knives or weapons.

I left hoping not to hear from these people again. After one month I had a call to my home and it was the mother of my student saying that the perpetrators had returned and there were seven of them, and that her son had run out after them with a baseball bat. I was stunned and also worried about what could happen to him as it could be a trap to lure him away so that they could take out their revenge on him. I rushed to the restaurant but he was not back and

I went searching for him and eventually I found him in a dead end, lying on the floor, lifeless. I called the police and it turned out that he was stabbed several times in the chest, back and even his groin. I was so angry and saddened that he had not listened to me. It hurt me so much seeing his parents' faces and their grief for their lost son — a waste of a life. They came to the west like me to have a better life and did not deserve this. I couldn't believe that there was no protection from such a cruel act of violence.

After two weeks the police arrested five of them and it went to court but we were told there was not enough evidence to convict them, as no weapons were recovered and they managed to produce alibis. I was shocked and horrified and asked myself if there is no justice, what could I do.

I was thinking about going after the people myself but my Master said that an eye for an eye makes the world blind and instead we needed to learn from this lesson. In my heart I had thought that this student could have been my successor and I was heartbroken losing him. I looked after the family for a while and no one came back to the restaurant to bully them.

Thinking back the world is full of injustice, the British always boast of human rights, yet where was the right for my student, the laws are meant to protect each and every one, yet where was the justice in this case. Yes I appreciate the freedom you get living here, but as foreigners I wondered if we were treated differently, I was confused.

Until now I was still seeking an answer. I finally found it through my human energy training, learning to connect my body, mind and soul. I found inner peace and I learned to forgive these people and I now understand I can't change the past. Those people will one day, be punished, not by me, but through Karma - what goes around comes around.

MY STUDENT DIANA

Teaching women martial arts in those days was rare, yet I welcomed them because I believed that the art is for all to enjoy regardless of sex, race and religion. I had a young lady called Diana who was very keen to learn. She was English so some of my Chinese students did not approve of her training with them. I told them we must not be prejudice against women and should train and work together to better each other's skills.

Thinking back it was a breakthrough to accept a woman into my Wing Chun school. I taught her differently because women's body and strength was different from men so I taught her the Gulao Wing Chun way so that if she was confronted by an attacker she would be able to handle herself.

After a year she had to go to Morocco for her work. After three weeks and while she was there I had a phone call from her saying she was nearly raped in the lifts and it was a very horrific experience. I asked her if she was okay and she told me that she entered the lift and had not realised that she was followed in by a member of management - she turned round and he was standing in front of her.

Once the lift door closed he had tried to put his arms round her and she froze instantly, my teachings sprang to her mind and she remembered that if she was confronted with an attacker to always remember chain punching and she did it - knocking him down. He was caught by surprise and she escaped - an action that saved her from a horrific ordeal.

She said that she understood now why I had reminded her to focus when punching whilst training in the Kwoon. This helped her in real life as once her mind was able to focus she could transfer what she had learnt into a real life situation. I was glad she was okay and told her to keep on practising the techniques I had taught her.

CHAPTER 10

Respect is Different Nowadays

The meaning of the title "Master"

RESPECT IS DIFFERENT NOWADAYS

Thinking back the respect to my Master in those days is unheard of nowadays. It is sad to see some students behave in an arrogant and disrespectful way, changing from master to master.

At that time my master was the only Wing Chun Master in the West, so there was no confusion in learning true martial arts, because only those who truly achieved master level could be authorised to teach. As I always said there are no bad students, only bad teachers that have created the current mess, as so many claim to be masters without understanding the meaning of the title, the art and the responsibility. Bad teaching will always create bad students making the art look bad.

To them it is just like business, they just pay and once they have their black sash they call themselves Masters or Grandmasters without any permission. Nevertheless I have to move on and accept that some people do behave like that but I also have many great and very respectful students all over the world.

A lot of students did not realize what I had to go through accepting all these challenges long before Wing Chun became popular thanks to my great kung fu uncle Bruce Lee in his movies. No one wanted to learn this art as it was "too soft" and was invented by a woman, it wasn't what men wanted to do. People from different styles used to criticize how bad the art looks, no power, too soft and not the kind of thing for a man to learn, they used to come down to my kwoon (school) in London Chinatown. Each time they were sent away by me - teaching them a lesson and I would be accused of using Thai boxing, Karate or Judo, not Wing Chun to defeat them.

They did not realize how powerful Wing Chun can be if one learns from a true master and then practises properly.

My master always said people used to say they learnt the ‚"original", "traditional" or the proper lineage in Wing Chun - what is the point claiming to be original or proper if it does not work for real. I have always believed that action speaks louder than words. That's why my Master and I were so close, because we both shared the same thinking and discipline.

There were some students who had been training under me for some time, and because of my travels due to my popularity working as a bodyguard and doing stunt work in the 70s and 80s,
I recommended some of my Chinese students to train with my master while I was away.

Unfortunately one or two lost the sense of respect to me because they thought that they were now at the same level as me in Wing Chun. There was one very cocky lad who had trained with my
master when I was away and kept boasting that his kung fu skills had overtaken mine and he could take me on in any fighting match.

Not knowing all this, I arrived back from Los Angeles and of course the first place I went was my master's restaurant to pay my respects. When I arrived I ordered my food and did not realise they were training at the backyard of the restaurant.

As I was eating my food one of the waiters told me that my Sifu wanted me to join them in the backyard. So I went to meet him. I greeted my master with respect and there were six of them training, five of whom used to train under me. Four greeted me with respect but one just ignored me and showed disrespect to me.

My master said that this guy had great potential and maybe his kung fu skills had exceeded mine. I told my master I was happy for this student, that he had improved whilst training with my master.

Then my Master told me to spar with that same student. I was exhausted after all those hours of travelling and without sleep, all I wanted right then was a bed to sleep on, not another sparring session.

However I could not say no to my master and in front of all the students I also needed to show them who I was.

As expected he came on hard and strong; in my mind I just wanted to finish it quickly, and when he rushed forward with his speed punching, I jumped away from him to the side, and jumped back with a side kick into his ribs - there was a cracking sound and he was down on the floor, screaming with pain, and the rest of the students were in shock.

My master looked at me with disgust for knocking down his student in that way. We had to call an ambulance; he had a cracked rib and had to stay in hospital for sometime.

After all that, when the ambulance had left, my master told me to chi sau with him, he asked me why I had used the kicking form technique on a fellow student. I told him I was sorry, I had done it because I was too tired and wanted to finish the fight as fast as possible.

He was angry that I had revealed the kicking form technique, which was not supposed to be shown at that time to anyone, and also quite angry with me for knocking his student down.

I apologised but he was still not happy, so during our chi sau training he hit me all over really hard. took it and I can still feel the pain now even after 30 years, he even elbowed me on my jaw, knocking out my back tooth too! What could I do? - he was my master. He taught me and looked after me, I had to take it and respect him.

THE MEANING OF THE TITLE "MASTER"

The title Master is being used by so many unqualified people. How have they managed to get this title? Who gave them the title? Nowadays people of all ages can call themselves a master without any authority. They spend a few months or a few years training abroad and then come back calling themselves a master. Opening training schools and teaching without understanding the art and the skill of teaching others; which not only ruins the art but the student too. Imagine training with someone for years and later finding out he was not genuine, how would you feel as a student when you had put your faith and trust in him? With so many people calling themselves ,"master" or ,"grandmaster" nowadays, it has become something that is of no importance.

People like me who have worked all their lives to reach the level feel that it has no meaning and it is degrading to the art and its principles. It's ok to open a school to start up a business but you must be true to yourself and the students, otherwise you can ruin the lives of others. That is why there are very few students of mine who are allowed to teach under my name because if they are not good enough I will not allow them to teach, but people nowadays have no idea what a master and student relationship really is.

Understanding the basic respect to the one who taught you is not known; once they get their black sash they are gone. Yet to me it's just the beginning of their journey.

People have now gone power mad wanting everything too quickly, opening schools all over the place just for financial gain, without any concern for other people's feelings. Let me define the word Master in Chinese (Sifu).

He is a man of great experience in his skills, knowledge and perfection of the art, after years of hard work and guidance he received from his master.

The title will be given to him once his master feels that he is the person who is morally able and kind enough to carry on the tradition of the art. By then he should possess the art of energy healing within himself after years of harnessing the art.

That is why I set a very high standard in my school; if a student has been training with me regularly for at least 15 years and has reached the age of 50, and wants to open a school under my name, then I might consider allowing them to do.

They will be tested by me regularly to make sure they are following the right path so that the art of Wing Chun can progress to the next generation and after.

If they decide after a while to go their own way (as we live in a free society which I embrace), then they will not be allowed to teach under my name. It took me a lifetime of sacrifice, hard work, dedication and nearly 45 years to reach my goal. I am not interested in quick financial gain to ruin it.

I am now approaching 60 years of age and my master did mention to me that this is the right age to be a Grandmaster in the art, yet to me the title is not important. Personally I am not interested in all these titles, I just want to teach and learn, and improve more, not only my martial art skills but also simply in being a human being on Mother Earth.

There are people nowadays who claim they had taught me this or that in my younger days, and want to make themselves feel superior to me, as I am now a well known master in martial arts worldwide - they just want to put me down.

To me this is childish; in those times I loved to train with lots of different martial artists to further my experience, and wanted to see how different styles work in order to further my skills. At the end of the day I did train in Malaysia with a few Taoist priests in the temple and my uncle in energy and martial arts, but most of my training skills and knowledge were taught to me by my Master Lee Shing. To me he was my only master and I am so grateful to have met him and learned from him.

The reason my master taught all his skills to me but not to others is because I believed in him and was always grateful for his kindness in teaching me and if ever there were problems, like challenges from others, I was always there. While most of his other students always made excuses not to be there, I am sure my master knew who was his true student not by words but by actions.

My popularity is not due to the fact that I trained with a famous master, or claim to be teaching the right lineage or original ways, but is due to my belief in showing the world what Wing Chun and Human Energy are, in a truthful way. My speed, power and martial arts perfection is not because I learned from a famous master, it is due to my own hard work, patience and dedication, and these have taken a whole life of sacrifice and dedication to achieve.

Now I just want to pass on these skills to the next generation.

CHAPTER 11

Incident with the East End Boys

A Problem with the Triad

Meeting the Triad's Boss

INCIDENT WITH THE EAST END BOYS

There were many incidents and one situation I can recall is four men from the the East End came in and I was told they were part of the "big boys" from there. They were rowdy and abusive to the waiter and refused to pay. Thinking of it now, it was crazy.

One of the waiters went downstairs and took a hammer and went behind one of the men and smashed it over his head! Either the man was drunk or had a hard head as I could see the hammer had just bounced off from his head. It was hilarious. He just stood up and grabbed the little waiter by the neck.

On seeing this, I did a side kick on his ribs knocking him over, his friends just froze and I shouted for them to pay or I would break their bones too on the spot; fortunately they paid and left. It was like something out of a Bruce Lee kung fu movie.

ALWAYS READY FOR ACTION

A PROBLEM WITH THE TRIAD

In another incident we had this so-called big triad's leader and their top fighter or "red pole" who claimed he was Yip Man's top fighter and was always slagging off my Master's Wing Chun skills. After a few times I decided to take action against him to shut his mouth once and for all. I asked for my Master's permission to challenge him to a fight.

My master approved and showed me how to handle him as he was huge for a Chinaman - 6 feet 4 and physically stronger than me. He must have added weight training in his programme. I went to him and challenged him and said if he did not accept they would have to leave the restaurant and never come back. Fearing loss of face he laughed and stood up towering over me and pushed me away immediately. I punched him on his nose so hard that I knocked him right down to the ground and he fell spreadeagled on his back.

I immediately stamped on his groin warning him if his boys tried to used weapons on me I would crush his nuts. They stopped and I ordered them to leave and never to return to the restaurant.

GUAN GONG, WORSHIPED BY THE TRIAD MEMBERS AS A SYMBOL OF POWER.

MEETING WITH THE TRIAD'S BOSS

The following day, news of this incident spread like wildfire and the head of the triad wanted an explanation from me and my Master. My Master and I decided that we would not step down; they had violated our good name and reputation. If we did that our position in Chinatown would be jeopardised.

The meeting was set on neutral ground in Chinatown, the Lido restaurant on Sunday evening at 6 pm, the year was 1976.
In order to prepare for the meeting my Master taught me double short stick fighting technique in case it turned nasty on that day. I carried two short steel sticks and one metal nunchaku with me,
I dressed in all black wearing two padded jackets thick enough to withstand any knives attacks. My Master wore a soft steel belt round his waist which could turn into a flexible steel sword - how cool was that.

Before we went to the restaurant we discussed how to deal with these people. We would not back down. I asked him what would happen if it turned bad. He said he would give me a sign. The signal was that he would turn the table over. That is when the action would start. Thinking about it, I am sure he must have had experienced this before as he wasn't even nervous talking about it.

It was a tense moment as my Master spoke for me because he was my elder and told them why I had to do that to his top man and would not step down. We were all Chinese away from home fighting each other, which was ridiculous.

They finally agreed that it was their mans bad behaviour that had led to this incident and that he had deserved to be taught a lesson not to behave in this manner in Chinatown, especially to my Master and me.

Thinking of this meeting even now makes my heart beat faster. I never like to see bullies, as having been a weak kid in school people tried to bully me.

That is why I trained my body so hard, to always protect myself and my family against all these sorts of people.

Since then no one dared to come to the restaurant to collect protection money or cause trouble. People were much better behaved and we did not have any more major incidents except a few drunken ones.

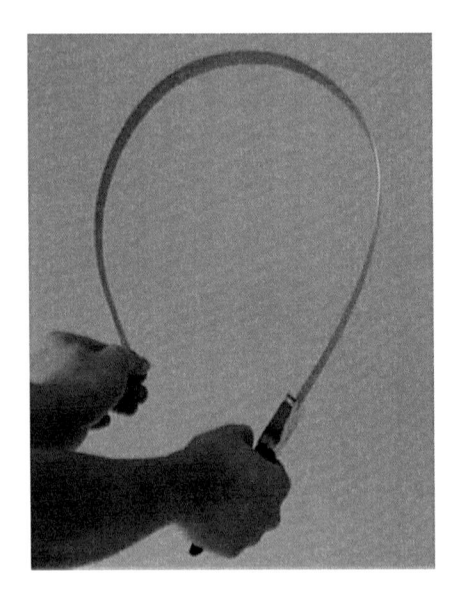

SIFU'S FLEXIBLE SWORD

CHAPTER 12

Working as a Bouncer

Problems with the Maltese

Dealing with 5 guys

WORKING AS A BOUNCER

Working in the French disco was also by chance. A friend of mine fell sick but could not find anyone to replace him and called me to help him temporarily. So I agreed to stand in for him, not realizing that the French owner preferred bigger guys to stand at the door. He was not happy to see a little guy like me.

PROBLEM WITH THE MALTESE

At that time in the seventies the Maltese were in control of all the sex shops in Soho. The two bosses were called Charlie and Freddie, they were friends of mine and all their boys used to come to my club (the French disco), having a good time whilst being respectful to me and the establishment.

One evening I was short of staff so I recruited a new bouncer just to help out as it was a busy Saturday evening. He came to the club and started bragging that he was a Thai boxing champion and had beaten many top free fighting masters. In those days we called it free fighting not mixed martial arts like nowadays. I explained to him not to be too cocky and to try to stay calm and be nice to the customers as we were dealing with things in a different way here and people might use knives and other weapons. And even guns, so it would be better to make friends with the customers. I sent him downstairs to keep an eye on things because I didn't normally go downstairs in those days. It was always full of smoke and smelt of cannabis - which I hated. At 2am the barman rushed upstairs and shouted to me that there was a major incident downstairs.

I went there straight away and in the corner I saw a group of people on top of someone, I immediately pulled them apart - most of them were the Maltese gang who knew me very well and respected me greatly, none of them dared try to have a go at me. The new bouncer was at the bottom, they were trying to suffocate him there and then. I pulled him up and asked him what happened, apparently he was trying to pick a fight with one of the Maltese boys and within seconds they were all on top of him. I told him how stupid he was and this was not the ring or the kwoon - there were no rules here.

DEALING WITH FIVE GUYS IN THE CLUB.

One evening the boss named Claude came up to the reception with five guys, I think they were Greek and Algerian. My boss had caught them stealing beer from the bars.

So I told them to go upstairs, and after reviewing the situation, I politely asked them to leave but my boss went crazy and started to swear at them calling them names.

Looking back at that moment he should have kept his mouth shut and let me handle them my way. One of the big guys threw a punch at Claude - seeing that, I instantly did a back fist on his cheek and knocked him over! At the same time I double kicked in the air, split kicked and knocked the two guys down.

SPLIT KICKING

The rest of the guys just stood there frozen. I shouted for them to leave and as they helped their friends up, they swore they would come back to sort me out. I got threats like those all the time so I took it with a pinch of salt. Claude was so impressed. He had now witnessed my skills and power so he promoted me to head bouncer.

In my heart I knew he'd doubted me all those other times not realising that he'd got the best looking after his interests.

After this incident I thought to myself in amazement at how I was so confident in myself this time. My master's teaching and my hard work had paid off, remembering in the past how I was so afraid when confronted by so many people, yet now I never even worried about my position. It made me feel great that I had improved my fighting skills to another level, that was all due to my master's teaching.

What I realised is that there is a huge difference between the real situation and training in school.

In true 70s style, they nicknamed me the baby faced assassin.

CHAPTER 13

Meeting Bruce Lee

Meeting Yip Chun

MEETING BRUCE LEE

In March 1973 my master told me to meet him in the restaurant because there was an important guest coming to see him. Not realising who that might be, I went to the restaurant.

When I arrived my Sifu, his wife, and a handful of my kung fu brothers were there. After 15 minutes a light blue Rolls Royce parked in front of the restaurant and out came the man himself!

He greeted my master with respect as he was his senior and said hello to me - we shook hands- to my mind he was a very charismatic and warm person.

They went to the back of the restaurant and my Simo prepared barbecued pork and noodles soup for him. He was there about 45 minutes and I was told he was on his way to Hong Kong.

After having a complete medical check up in Los Angeles, he had been given the all clear and was in good health. It was a great shock to all of us when we heard that he died on July 20th 1973 in Hong Kong.

I asked my Sifu how could that happen to a man who had been declared physically fit and in good health, and then suddenly he just dies? He said that when Bruce Lee came to him, he wanted to know more about the internal training art of Wing Chun and Chi Kung.

He said that if a human keeps pushing his external physical strength too far then the internal organs will not be able to support it and the body will just give up one day resulting in death.

He also said that in Wing Chun training a student must learn to balance the physical body and the internal energy, if they don't it will result in imbalance in the body.

I was too young to understand it at that time but now it is clear to me in all martial arts training, one needs to learn to balance oneself to maintain a strong physical and internal body.

We all paid our respects to Bruce Lee and in my heart I thank him for introducing Wing Chun to the world.

MEETING YIP CHUN

Yip Chun came to London in 1982 to visit my master and stay in his home. I was responsible for taking him around and looking after him, for three weeks. He was a small guy, around 5 ft 2, and slim.

He was also easy to get along with, he enjoyed Chinese food and smoking his pipe. I did a demonstration in honour of him in front of my master and himself.

When he left he signed and presented me with a certificate as a life long member of the Yip Man Association.

CHAPTER 14

My Travels

TV's Just Amazing

Breaking the Guinness World Record

MY TRAVELS

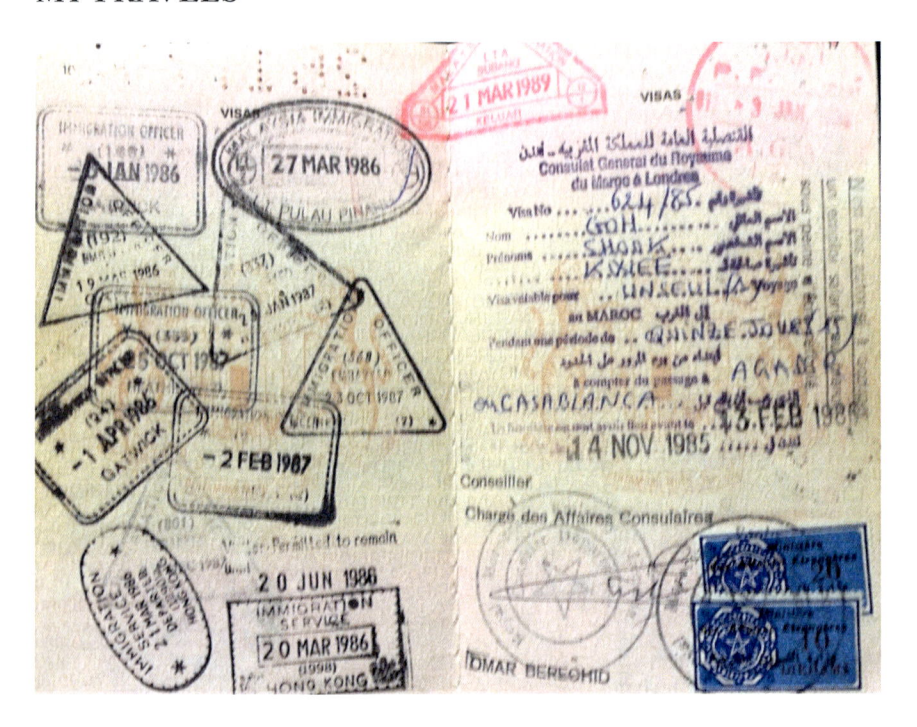

In 1976 I was invited to Germany, Switzerland, Scandinavia and Russia as a good will tour to promote Wing Chun and Chi Kung. It was a eye opener for the public, as they had never seen Chinese martial arts. After a successful tour we were invited to tour the United States and South America.

At that time it was big news and I was treated like a rock star. What an amazing experience. The place that I fell in love with was Hawaii, it was so beautiful and the people were so friendly and helpful. I told myself if I ever wanted to retire that would be the place.

One of my travels that was most disappointing was my trip to China in 1986. I had heard of a Chi Kung Master that could project his Chi onto any attacker and then use his Chi to push him away without touching him. Before I took the trip I asked my master's opinion, does such a person exist in China any more?

We had a lengthy conversation and he told me to go to experience it. He had heard of such masters in his time in China but never witnessed it himself so he gave me permission to go. I was excited that my master allowed me to go but also a bit sceptical.

Eventually I arrived in China and found the master. He lived in the Canton province, famous for all sorts of martial arts training styles. I was so excited because I thought if I can master this, it will be great for me in my bodyguard work.

FILMING IN HAWAII

I agreed to pay him 2000 US dollars, a lot of money in those days - nowadays it would be more like 30,000 dollars yet the fee did not deter me. Before we started training I asked the master to demonstrate on me. So I walked towards him six times but each time he failed to push me away with his Chi. I was so upset, I was so disappointed but didn't give up. I told him maybe he was too tired on the day so I would come again the next day.

The next day I went there in the afternoon but this time the master was not there - his student just made an excuse for him that he had to go away. Eventually I left and went back to London to report to my Sifu regarding my experience in China.

When I told him he just laughed and said all great masters had left China during the communist takeover. Real kung fu was banned, only wushu was taught, just for basic health.
The communist regime forbade any fighting martial arts fearing that those people who practised them might rebel against it. He said that there was no special kung fu but only hard work, dedication and learning under a true master then you can succeed..

After that I went to visit Chee Kim Tong, who at that time was the Grand Master of Shaolin kung fu in Malaysia, to seek advice on martial training. When I met him, to show my respect, I presented him with a jade, engraved with his name, which I had specially made for him. He had heard about my master and Yip Man; in those days this was a huge compliment as they were not that well known, like nowadays.

I performed Wing Chun in front of him, and my chi kung, which he was very impressed with and I also demonstrated my inch punch and speed punch. He was so impressed he told me I was the future grandmaster of the Wing Chun clan. I thanked him for his kind words before I left to go to the States.

I had many experiences like this, meeting many masters from different styles, sparring and learning how the different styles work. It was eye-opening, and through these experiences, I got a bigger and better understanding of how Wing Chun can be used to deal with different situations.

MY STUNTWORKS HIT THE HEADLINE IN ASIA

TV'S JUST AMAZING 1984

As I became more famous in England, one TV producer heard about me and wanted me to appear on a popular programme called "Just Amazing". It was hosted by the late world motorcycle champion Barry Sheen and famous TV actor Kenny Lynch. To me it was an honour to share the same stage with such legends, they were very friendly and helpful to me during rehearsal.

I was at ease and did a great demonstration of my hard chi kung skills, like having bricks placed on my arms, shins, and groin, to be smashed by a sledgehammer wielded by one of my students. I even bent two iron rods which were placed on my throat, to demonstrate hard chi kung technique.

It was mind-blowing for the audience to see, as I was the first person ever to show all these skills on British television - after this the audience nicknamed me ,"the Iron Man of Wing Chun". The audience were also stunned to see me lie down, have two concrete blocks placed against the side of my head, then my student smashed the blocks with the sledgehammer.

GUINNESS WORLD RECORDS 2001

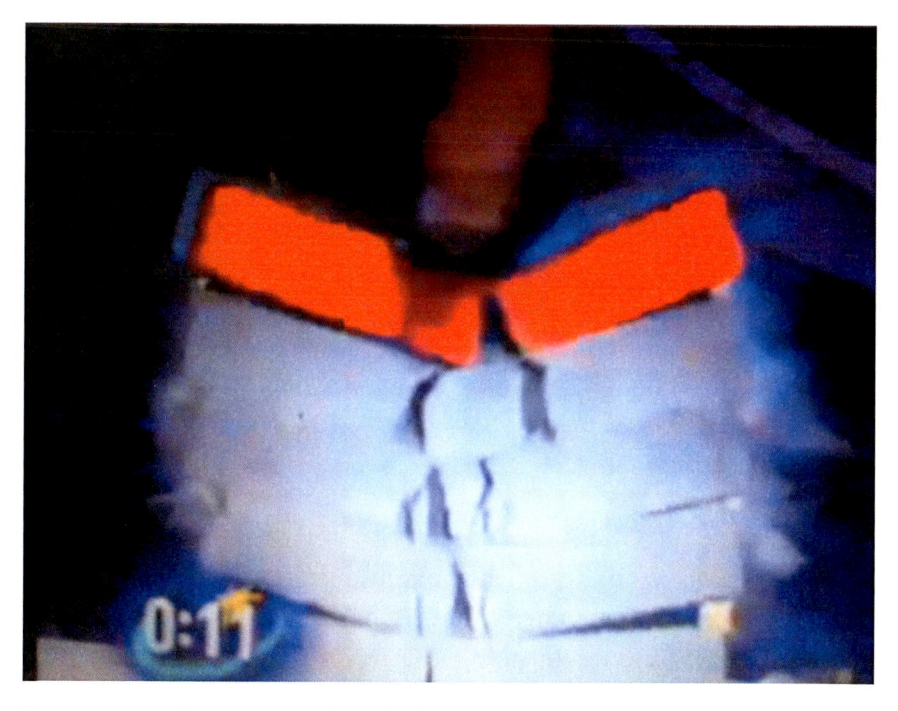

I was invited to try to break the world record for concrete block breaking on ITV, it was an honour as many had attempted but failed. I had to break all the concrete blocks with my left arm. As we were preparing for the live show in the evening I arrived with my students during the day to rehearse - it was hard because doing it on TV was a whole new world - the director wanted me to break it at different angles that suited the camera shots. I had to stop and start a few times because either the cameramen were not ready or the lights were not right.

It is so different in a martial arts demonstration, where you can concentrate on your own with no camera or director telling you what to do. I kept calm and made sure my body was warm so that

I would be ready when they decided for me to go ahead to break the record. Finally the moment arrived, instantly I blocked myself mentally from the audience, lights, cameras and director so that I could concentrate on breaking the record. I took a deep breath and started smashing the concrete blocks, it took me 11 seconds to do it. It was unbelievable - I did it and the audience went crazy. After breaking the first record I attempted to break another record by placing 15 concrete blocks on my stomach and my student broke the concrete blocks on my stomach with a sledgehammer.

It was hard as the weight of the concrete placed on my body felt like a baby elephant on top of me! I used my hard chi kung breathing technique to control the pain and absorb the impact of the sledgehammer smashing on my body.
It was tough but I did it.

I was the only man ever to attempt two records in one night. These were unforgettable moments for me.

CHAPTER 15

Bodyguard and Stuntman

BODY GUARD AND STUNTMAN

In 1980 I met a young prince from Qatar. It was fate or coincidence that morning, 3am as usual as I went out to close the club and while I was on the street, I saw a big red Bentley coming down the street. A very rare sight in those days; in my heart I thought this guy must be filthy rich. He parked the car just opposite my club and as he was coming out he was confronted by four Jamaican guys.

In those days Soho was controlled by the Jamaican gangs selling their drugs but most of them knew me or had heard of me. I saw the situation and went over to help him, when the four men saw me I just told them that he was my friend and they left him alone.
I told him it was crazy to be in this part of London with an expensive car, he said he was lost and wanted to go back to Knightsbridge.

Before he went he was curious as to how I had the power to tell these people to leave him alone. I told him what I did there and that most of these people knew me and respected my work. Later we became great friends and he wanted me to look after him.

In our travels we went all over the world - what a life the other half live! People can have too much money. It was an eye opener for me when we were in Hollywood.

I did stunts in a few movies and I met so many up and coming actors, actresses, and directors like Spielberg, George Lucas, Cameron and was chosen to act as stunt double in a movie about my kung fu uncle the great Bruce Lee.

At that time I was called the Bruce Lee of England. I spent three years away and had enough, I just wanted to get my life back doing things that I want and also to start teaching Wing Chun and Human Energy.

The decision was made for me in one major incident as some of my prince's friends' bodyguards were much bigger than me and arrogant. They started to make fun that I was too small to even block a bullet. To my mind I was not there to block bullets with my body but to protect the young prince. This body guard was at least 6 feet 6 inches tall with his biceps bigger than my head!

One day he came over and started bad mouthing and wanted to bet with me for 10,000 dollars that he would easily take me apart with his bare hands. I was so angry at that time and had had enough of his insults and in front of the rest of the people there I accepted the bet there and then.

As we stood facing each other it was like a 6 year old standing up to a grown adult; thinking back my Master always said every human has its weak points - size can have advantages but the bigger they are the harder they fall. In order to knock out a bigger opponent you need speed, then followed by chi power not physical power.

KICKING WITH POWER AND PRECISION

Remembering that I took a deep breath and as he tried to punch me, I turned and did a turning side kick on his knee so fast that no one could see it coming. I heard a loud crack and a big scream, as I turned around he was on the floor crying in pain. It took four big guys to lift him up to go to the hospital. I heard I had broken his knee and he couldn't walk with that leg again.

After a week or two, my closest bodyguard friends told me that his mates were looking for revenge and might come after me with weapons; fearing this I decided to leave America and came back to England. I kept a low profile for a while until the incident in the States blew over.

I decided I had had enough of the bodyguard and bouncer's life. Sometimes I wonder is it me? Am I a trouble maker? Why did I not walk away from all these fights?! But how could I have? It was my job, my choice. I believe we should all respect one another regarding race, religion, culture, or size, but it's not that way for some.

We humans can be so bad to one another, especially some men who think that size can push people around but these people also contributed to the way I am now- making me train harder to increase the level of my kung fu, speed and power.

CHAPTER 16

Opening a Martial Arts Shop

MY MARTIAL ARTS SHOP IN CARNABY STREET, LONDON (1984)

SELLING WEAPONS IN THE SHOP

When I arrived back in London I decided to open a martial arts shop. The shop which was in Carnaby Street attracted lots of different people from all walks of life. I had the racist National Front, the skinheads, the triads, and the football hooligans coming to buy all sorts of weapons like nunchaku, ninja stars, coshes (extendable batons), and balisong knives.

All the above mentioned people had nothing to do with martial arts - it was just crazy how people behaved in there. During football season all these so-called football fans from Milwall, Chelsea, and elsewhere came in and bought lots of ninja stars and coshes so that they could use them for hurting others; it was madness. The triads were into samurai swords and the skinheads were into knuckledusters. The punks were into coshes but to me it was all good business.

The shop attracted lots of ruffians, tough guys and mad people because they all wanted weapons for whatever reasons they may have had. Fights broke out all the time in the shop and I had to establish myself as the tough boss of the shop and stood my ground against any threats.

One time a skinhead came into the shop and took an extendable baton and smashed it on his friend's head and it broke, then he told me this was crap and cheap, but I told him if he did not pay no way could he leave the shop. He refused at first, so I snatched the broken baton off the floor and stabbed it into his groin. It was painful, I could see it on his face.

Then I grabbed his ear and twisted it and told him to pay or he could leave his ear with me as payment. He told me to take the purse out of his pocket and take the money. I did that and told him to leave my shop.

My reputation grew and people who came to the shop always behaved themselves when they came inside, whoever they were. I earned their respect - maybe the hard way. Until one day they went too far using their weapons. On the BBC 6 o'clock news, the nation was horrified to see fans being hit by the ninja stars and beaten by coshes, it was bad news and the authorities started to crack down on all these weapons, eventually banning them.

Even after they banned the selling of weapons from my shop, still some people would come in to try to buy them.
There was one time four black guys came in and insisted on buying some weapons and I told them nicely that I didn't sell them anymore. They became angry and started swearing at me and refusing to go, insulting me and my family - that was my last straw. I kicked one in the knee and punched the other one, and they fell out of the shop onto the street, and were lying there crying with pain, while the other two ran out of the shop and stood there accusing me of being racist towards them.

The police arrived as the crowd gathered round. I was handcuffed and led away and taken to West End Central police station. It was hilarious because most of the guys who worked there were my students - I was in there for 24 hours and there was no case to answer, as those boys were crooks and did not come forward to press any charges against me. Thinking back I wonder was I right to sell all those things to the public or was I showing my dark side? I had lost my moral compass and my beliefs just for money. Maybe I did go to the dark side of my life for a while by behaving like this, nevertheless it was also part of learning and experience, the journey of my life.

CHAPTER 17

My Darkest Period

Being Ambushed

Healing from my Master

MY DARKEST PERIOD

Even though business was good there were too many expenses like wages, bills, rent, tax and others. Though money was coming in, it went out as quickly paying all these things. I was also wholesaling my products and giving away hundreds of thousands in credit to people. More than half ran away and some even declared bankruptcy so I lost a lot of money. I was also into properties buying and selling but unfortunately when the property crash came I was in a mess and it affected my family and me greatly. I owed millions to the banks and could not support the loans because most of the properties I had were empty and there were not enough tenants paying the rent to service the bank.

All my so called friends deserted me and I also had problems with my family. I was lost not knowing what to do, my master was not around as he had gone to Canada, I had no one to turn to. I was heart broken but I bit the bullet and got on with it. Luckily my Prince from Qatar heard about my financial problems and helped me out.

I managed to get rid of the properties but with a lower price and the bank and came to a compromise: to pay back the loan.
In Chinese culture, sharing this and telling everybody that you are a failure is a loss of face. But to me it's a lesson and a reality check where you know who your real friends and family are. A big lesson for me.

There also were publishers who published my books and were refusing to pay me any royalties. I thought to myself "why are people behaving like this?". People and some students of mine whom I had helped to set up their school abroad had also turned against me after they established themselves.

Not only did they not want to know me, some even said that my kung fu was not original and I was only making things up as I went along. I asked myself what had I done wrong? Yet still no one helped me except for my master and a few friends. After all this misfortune I decided not to teach openly for a while.

I went away for sometime, just to reflect on all of this, how I could start again. Eventually I said to myself that I am a man of martial arts and great discipline, nothing can stop me from coming back. All great people always come back and I will do the same. I started again slowly and then I felt better within myself and more careful with people who wanted to exploit me.

I have forgiven those who had done me wrong as now I am a true disciple of Tao. I believe in karma too and because of my beliefs I am always willing to help people without wanting anything in return. I have lots of great people who help me and encourage me and these people truly are my heroes. These people I thank from the bottom of my heart.

Being naive and trusting people so easily, perhaps I always have had a kind heart and think that everybody is like me. This time I have truly grown up. What an experience but it so sad to treat people like this because we should help one another instead of hurting each other. This is the real world, at one point when I left my family's home, I turned round and the saw the expression on the face of my youngest son; it was so upsetting! Nothing I can do to reverse everything I did wrong but after nearly 10 years I managed to pick myself up slowly but surely.

Life is a journey of up and down we need to learn to cherish the good times and overcome the bad times.

BEING AMBUSHED

I remember it clearly it was 4 am, after I'd finished at my job I walked towards Chinatown and felt someone approaching me, as I turned around I felt a bottle smash on my forehead and then my head was streaming with blood, pouring into my eyes. I was blinded for a second and felt someone stabbing the broken bottle into my stomach. In an instant I grabbed his arms and twisted them as hard as I could, I could hear him screaming with pain and calling for help from his friends. The next moment I felt a baseball bat smash into my knee! It was painful but bearable... luckily I had my trusty nunchaku with me. I managed to wipe the blood from my eyes and started swinging the nunchaku around, knocking two of the guys down and the one who smashed me with the bottle. Moments later I could see a car with flashing lights, it was the police!

They came in time but one of the men managed to run away. I thought I took three down - it turned out that there were four of them lying on the ground in Greek Street. I sat on the ground putting my shirt on my forehead to stop the bleeding. An ambulance finally arrived and took us all to the hospital. I had nearly sixty stitches on my forehead and was told I might not be able to walk properly again. I stayed in hospital for three days - after being interviewed by the police I was told three of the guys had broken jaws and one had broken arms and a fractured skull from my nunchaku attack.

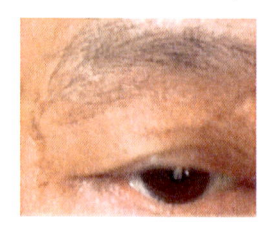

SCARS STILL VISIBLE AFTER 35 YEARS

I realised these were the same five guys who had threatened to sort me out several weeks before in the club. I was told I might be charged for GBH - grievous bodily harm, a serious offence. I told them I was only defending myself as those guys had been trying to kill me. We went to court but I was acquitted as they never showed up to court - it was believed they all had a few criminal records themselves.

This was not the first time I was ambushed, it had happened a few times but each time I was prepared and took care of it. A lot of people did not realize how tough my life was and some of my friends thought it was a joke if I ever told them what had happened to me, they thought I was making it up.

Until one afternoon as I was walking to my kwoon someone just jumped out from the corner and tried to grab me from behind- quick as a flash I elbowed him and I heard a crack as he fell down, there was blood all over his face. When I looked closer it was my bouncer friend and he always thought that I made up stories regarding my fight incidents.

I felt so bad - he should not have done that. I called the ambulance and he was in hospital for nearly a month with a broken jaw and arms. I told him what he had done was stupid and now he might understand how my life was, I was always alert and prepared for anything.

Looking back I was lucky that my hard and tough training over the years saved my life. I used to practise to toughen my forehead with a metal ruler and use chi to remove the internal injuries and bruises inside the brain - this training is not recommended for most people.

HEALING FROM MY MASTER

After my injury the first person I went to see was my master, to seek help for healing on my knee. It was amazing, he sent his energy down to the area of pain and I felt a warm sensation entering my knee, and then most of what had been swollen, had subsided and the pain was reduced greatly. I could not believe it. I had studied science and physics. How could someone just put their palms on the pain and take it away? I was blown away and asked him what type of chi kung was this?

Reluctantly he told me this chi kung training had been almost completely destroyed by the communists which is why many masters with this skill escaped from China fearing they would be prosecuted if they were found out to possess this skill. He made me promise him that if he taught me this art I would have to swear not to show it to anyone. And only at least ten years after he died, then could I openly show or teach it to people.

Of course I promised. I had to kneel down in front of him and swear to heaven and earth that I would honour my Master's wish.

CHAPTER 18

Training Human Energy

TRAINING HUMAN ENERGY

Once you start to train human energy you must learn to be patient and practise it regularly and you need to carry on with your training especially on level one because this will strengthen your foundation. It will take another five years then your chi will reach maturity like a boy turning into a man. You must understand that energy training is not like training in kung fu. You just need to practise it regularly and you can perfect it, but human energy it takes time to cultivate and harness it, so be a bit patient and you will reach your goal.

Let me share with you the basic breathing exercises

1. Breathing through your lungs:
Breathe slowly and deeply through your nose while envisaging filling your lungs from top to bottom, hold it for 5 seconds then exhale through your mouth.

2. Breathing using your stomach muscles
Breathe slowly into the lungs and place both palms on your stomach. Press the stomach inward and hold for 5 seconds then breathe out through your mouth. Practise this regularly 3 to 5 times a day then you will find that your lungs will be much stronger.

It was proven through scientific research that cancer cells cannot survive in high levels of oxygen. But it would be naive to presume that simply controlling your breathing could act as a preventive measure or a cure.

Cancer cells use oxygen and produce energy differently from healthy cells. Cancer is caused by damaged cells growing out of control due to a bad lifestyle or environmental factors, faulty metabolism is an effect of this process rather than a cause.

There's no scientific evidence that deep breathing with normal air can prevent or treat cancer however if one can learn to breathe properly it will enhance the nervous system which can slow down the heart beat, improve respiratory and cardiovascular function, decrease the effect of stress and improve physical and mental health. This will reduce the chances of cancer.

In other words learn to control your breath rather than let it control you. In order to maintain good health, not only must you learn to breathe properly, you also need to balance your lifestyle. Rest, diet and regular practiceing of the human energy programme will all help you to do this.

Training human energy was something of an eye opener. All my thoughts of being a tough guy like wanting to push more weights and hard physical training was out of the window. I have to learn to relax myself from top to bottom by just practising the three vibrating hands.

To my surprise I found it quite difficult and very tiring practising it after fifteen minutes it was surprising to me as I could easily spar in a full contact session for a hour without being tired but by practising this I could feel the pain deep in my body. I asked my master how this could be. He told me that in order for the human body to be strong internally, one needs to learn to have a good circulation and that takes time and patience. Most students of martial arts are solely into exercising the external part of the body therefore by causing imbalance.

I had heard hin say that before, but did not take notice Only after getting hurt and then receiving healing from him - then only it woke me up and opened my eyes to see further. Than just trying to strengthen myself with weights and hard physical training.

I preserved and followed his instruction to the letter. Once I felt the chi on my palms and in my body it was an incredible feeling, a feeling of euphoria, calm and inner peace. One cannot describe how it feels when the chi touches your soul - it was mind blowing.

After that I was far calmer and in sparring sessions I seemed to be much faster and every technique was executed with precision. It was an amazing feeling being able to knock my opponent down with so little effort.

I always remember the first human energy training session with my Master was something that I could not have imagined. When I arrived at his house he gave me a bag of rice covered in canvas, about six inches by six inches, and around three inches thick, weighing at least eight pounds. What he told me truly sank my heart.

He told me to take the bag of rice home and place it on a solid table and use my five fingers only, to hit the bag until it all turned to powder. I was looking forward to starting my energy training with him so was shocked to hear that this was my task. However, I did what he told me. Upon leaving I asked how long he thought it would take and he replied that it would be about six months and once it had all turned to powder to bring it back. I shrugged, accepted my task and went home.

First I spent five hours non-stop using the fingers of both hands and striking it as hard as I could. It was so painful, the next day all my fingers were swollen and bleeding. I told myself "I can't do this"; it would kill me long before the rice turned to powder. I tried to think of another way and finally I thought I could use my fists and feet - that should do the trick.

After three months I could feel the rice had all turned to powder so I took it back to my Master. He looked surprised and said that it was great that I had done it in three months; half the time he anticipated.

He cut open the bag with a knife and all the powder poured to the ground in his garden. He looked at it, and then felt the powder in his fingers and turned round looking stern and angry. I asked him if it was good enough and he wanted to know how I hit the rice into powder. I replied with my fingers, but immediately he detected my lie and his voice was strong so I admitted that I had used my fists and feet to do it.

He then asked if I wanted to succeed in energy training. I said yes of course. He responded by saying "then don't lie to me ever again" and if I still wanted to train in energy healing then I must do exactly as instructed. He told me that he would give me one last chance and handed me another bag of rice and once again told me to use my fingers to hit it until it turned to powder. I left feeling guilty and ashamed about lying to him and regretful about not following his instruction to the letter.

For the next six months I hit the bag every day and even took it to bed as I was so determined to succeed and eventually it did all turn to powder.

The first three months nearly killed me but I kept on hitting it with my fingers, they were so bruised and the pain sometimes unbearable. It was like being in a kung fu movie, I couldn't even hold chopsticks together, yet I did not give up. When I did my press up, weight training, sparring and bag work it hurt, but even that doesn't compare to the pain I felt with this training.

When I took the bag to my master he did the same as before, cut it open and felt the powder on his fingers, he placed it in his mouth and then turned around and said well done. When he said that, I felt that a ton of weight came off my shoulders. I asked him why I had needed to do that and he said that to practise energy healing is on a completely different level.

This time he handed me another bag, but this one was full of marbles and he said that I could use my palms and knuckles but not my feet to hit it until it all turned to powder. This time I did what he told me and did it in three months; it was hard work but again I was determined, and so I persevered.

Warning - Do not attempt to practise this. It can be damaging to your hands and fingers. If you want to train like this then make sure the person who teaches you know what is he teaching.

Upon seeing that I had completed my task he then explained that in order to be an energy master one must have strong fingers, palms and fists for the pressure points techniques in healing and in fighting the Dim Mak way (the highest pressure points fighting technique.)

The next level in chi training was to practise my three vibrating hands technique which I named the "A B C" technique. The reason for doing this is to build up good circulation, opening up all the channels and loosening the joints so the chi will flow round the body faster and more strongly. Therefore, the chance of achieving healing power increase greatly.

Practising the three vibrating hands could be tough and exhausting I felt my hands were going to fall off, it's was tough how I felt at that time. I did it in the rain, snow and sun, all year round so that my body and mind could cope with all the different weather in order for the body to increase my chi power for fighting and healing. After 5 years I felt so much stronger within my body and the tingling sensation had increased greatly. It was an amazing feeling. No one could understand how I felt so wonderful and calm now. Only then I understood the basic feeling of chi in ones body.

I practised the three vibrating hands technique and the healing form for the next 15 years, finally finishing level 1 to 8. It was such an experience, so different from my training in Wing Chun; every different technique in energy work must be carried out in a relaxed precise and calm way. It was not easy at first but after a while I found that the more I trained, the calmer I became, and my power in punching and even kicking had increased greatly.

It was surprising but welcome. I could feel my palms and body tingling with chi; it was such an wonderful feeling and one I had never felt before. It gave me a sense of calm and inner peace within my mind and soul. I felt more happy now in my human energy training with my master, and grateful that he guided me in the right direction.

After fifteen years I wanted to go further with my energy training, I wanted to be like my Master, to be an energy healer like him so I decided to help a few of my friends and it was a great success. I was happy and went even further helping someone who had leukaemia. They felt better but after five days I felt that all my energy had been drained away, I was tired all the time. I had a headache and felt sleepy all the time and ill. I did not understand how come I felt like that, I thought to myself "I am usually always fit, active and strong" - so I went to the doctor who said that I probably had a virus attack a sort of flu, so he gave me lots of tablets for it. I did not take any as I did not want to harm my body further. I know that the side effects outweigh the cure. Eventually I went to seek my Master for healing. The moment he saw me he said that my chi had been depleted and asked me what I had been doing. I told him I had been healing others and he was very angry saying that I was jeopardising my health and life by doing that, as my body was not strong enough to do that because the chi had not matured and was not strong enough to heal others. My body would absorb all the bad energy and if I did not have the ability to get rid of it, then it would harm me and the consequence could be fatal.

After that he placed his palm on my Tan Tien (life force area) just below my navel. Immediately I felt heat goes into my body and after twenty minutes I felt warm all over and the pain, the discomfort seemed to flow upward and it was like out of the body experience, I felt so good and calm. I will never forget this feeling for the rest of my life. When he finished he gave me a glass of warm water to drink, he told me that the warm water would help the chi to flow better and told me not to do any healing. I was not ready for it and I must be patient, and my time would come when I was ready.

I was so happy and lucky to have a master like him not only did he teach me his amazing skill, he even saved my life and I did not know how to repay him. I thought to myself that I would do whatever he wanted me to do and hopefully learn it properly. This lesson had made me wiser and more patient in my life.
I have now designed an easy to learn programme, to share my knowledge with anyone wanting to learn about this amazing energy so that students do not make the same mistake as me.

WHY I FELT SICK AFTER HEALING A CANCER PATIENT

People suffer cancer of all types because their immune system have been attacked by the cancer cells, causing organs to shut down and extinguishing the life force, potentially resulting in death.

So if a Master who possesses healing energy (life force) uses his life force with a cancer patient, he will pass on his hard earned healing energy to them and absorb all the patient's negative energy, so once the healer loses all his energy through healing, he needs to firstly release all the negative energy that he has absorbed and then he will have to go back to his Master and nature to replace all the lost energy. By learning to meditate through deep slow and calm breathing techniques he can replace all lost energy. This is essential to maintain the healer's own health.

WHAT IS LIFE FORCE ?

Each and every living thing has life force - it is the energy that determines how long we can live and it varies from one to another, some are born with a longer and some with a shorter life force. In this century it is believed that through our advancement in medical science and technology, that we are living longer but in reality, thousands of years ago people still lived into their eighties and beyond. So I am curious to know if the human race has actually extended their life span through science.

In my opinion I doubt it, both my grandparents lived into their nineties and my mum is in her eighties, and in those days people had lots of children too without the help of medicine. The big difference to me is that the air and food they had were much cleaner and the food contained far less chemicals compared to today. So my assumption is that a less polluted air and natural food environment might be the key to give us all a longer, healthier life in addition to learning to maintain a good circulation daily.

Life force is stored in your Tan Tien (just below your navel and is about the size of your fist) therefore it is important to learn to maintain it through proper breathing so that it will not be depleted due to daily work, as this can result in stress and strain, damaging your life force and potentially leading to disease.

CHAPTER 19

History of Human Energy

Principles of Human Energy

HISTORY OF HUMAN ENERGY

The art of chi healing has been passed down for centuries through the Chinese masters. In China today energy healing plays a key part in modern healing practices and is becoming increasingly recognised in the west, however here there is a barrier of skepticism surrounding alternative practices. I am committed to working with the scientific community to document the significant physical changes produced by chi healing. Hopefully this will help to convince the skeptics that chi healing does actually work.

Chi kung exercises were developed by Taoists over 2500 years ago. They all have a common purpose which is to attempt to transform the natural energy of chi, found throughout the universe, into a form which can be of good use to boost the human body for a long and healthy life.

This energy can be absorbed from the outside, compressed, stored, and used in different ways within the body. Soft exercises are practised to move chi around the body in order to clear energy blockages. The free flow of chi to all internal tissues and organs will promote good health

As there are so many types of chi kung exercises developed over the years I found it confusing and no one can practise all of it. Some consist of too many complicated movements, techniques which might take ten lifetimes to learn. I therefore decided to simplify the chi kung training programme in order to make it easier to understand and so that you can learn it in a simple manner.

I call it the Human Energy Training Programme.

PRINCIPLES OF HUMAN ENERGY

In Human Energy, the key to a long and healthy life is to learn to have a balance lifestye. There might be some confusion as to how to do it. People might say "I work, exercise, eat healthily is that not enough?"

Being healthy and disease free is not just that; it is important to learn how to connect your body and mind. The question is how to do this? Isn't it good enough not to smoke or drink and always live a healthy lifestyle. I would like to share with you what I mean by connecting body and mind, because through my years of training experience with my master I realise that for a human body and mind to connect, one needs to learn to breathe properly - that is, always breathe in through your nose to receive good oxygen, and breathe out through your mouth to release all the bad air or energy. Then you practised this regularly for sometime, then o your lungs will be clear and strong. This is follow by the three vibrating hands technique to improve your circulation.

Once you have done that you move on to cupping (gently hitting with the hand held in a cup shape) to awaken the energy in your muscles and bones.

The next step is to learn to release your negative energy through the sounds "Ha" (to release physical pain) and "He" (to release emotional pain).

The principle of Human Energy is to learn to have a good circulation round your body and then the body will be ready to connect with the mind. You do not need to learn all about the human body in detail like all the 360 pressure points connecting to the various organs, as in my experience I find this unnecessary and confusing. The mind will not be able to absorb or remember all of this information in a short time. Therefore the less, the better.

We just need to know where our lungs, liver, kidneys, heart and stomach are in our body. This I am sure is quite simple to learn.
All these organs need to work in harmony together to make you healthy. Once you learn about them you will realise how important it is to know how these organs work within the body.

The lungs receive and expel air, the liver stores our proteins and detoxifies, the kidneys act as a filter to rid of our liquid waste. The heart pumps good blood round our body and the stomach digests all food into glucose for energy in our cells.

Once you have a basic understanding of how your body works then you can learn the art of connecting your body and mind. Your organs will work in harmony within your body and then you can move on by learning to connect with nature helping you to strengthen your body further.

CHAPTER 20

Human Energy Programme

Conversation with my Master

HUMAN ENERGY PROGRAMME

Human Energy is based on the ancient Chinese art of Chi Kung which was the precursor to the martial arts. If one trains Human Energy it will not only improve their health but it will also complement their martial arts skill and take their training to a higher level.

With this in mind I have designed an easy to learn, three year programme for anyone wishing to train Human Energy and become a certified practitioner. Students will learn to collect, balance and maintain their energy for a long and fruitful life. The programme I have designed has eight levels and can be learnt within three years of practice:

LEVEL 1 (CONNECTING WITHIN ONESELF)
Students are introduced to Chi. Chi is your life force within your body and by practising, cultivating and harnessing and following the programme you will achieve your goal. A key focus at this level is to improve your blood circulation which helps the energy (chi) to flow around the body without restriction. This allows a student

to achieve a good chi flow and enables you to strengthen your life force - sometimes referred to as your energy ball. In this level I will project my energy to firstly help you to improve your circulation, rid of all pain - physical and emotional as well as any health issues. Some students will have cold hands.

This means that their blood circulation round their body has been blocked and needs to be unblocked. For some who feel nausea or sickness, then it will be the liver that is full of toxins which needs to be released first. If they feel light headed then the circulation to the head is blocked. Fatigue or lack of energy is due to bad circulation and finally if they feel out of breath there is problem with their heart.

I will advise them to practise the five breath follow by the three vibration hands and the "ha" and "he" sounds, to release all negative energy out and to improve their circulation first. Start with ten minutes first for at least three months. Once all these symptoms have subsided, or in other words the circulation has improved; then they can move on with their training.

Therefore energy training can be very dangerous if the master does not know what he is teaching because it can do more harm then good to the student. That is why learning energy techniques is a serious matter and you must make sure you find the right master, because if you are not ready to learn the more advanced techniques then the result can be damaging to your health.

There were many cases where the students had felt the chi on their palms and on their faces while practising with me in class, yet when they go back home and no matter how much they try, they don't experience the same feeling of chi on them. I can explain that when they are in my class I am projecting my energy to them helping and healing them. It is hard for people nowadays to understand this, how can it be that some one without even touching you can send his energy to you? That sounds too far fetched.

There are so many skeptics because it is not easy to find a true master of energy nowadays as it takes years of training, cultivating harnessing and receiving energy from a master in a gradual way so that the body mind and soul can absorb it and that takes years of training.

I can only explain it like this: if a baby only require three bottles of milk a day but you feed the baby with five bottles does it make the baby grow faster and bigger? I don't think so, not it will only harm the baby but. That is why to me the student must learn to practise and understand level one thoroughly and if they don't I will not allow them to move on to the next level.

That is why in ancient times in China, students who studied energy work always stayed and practised with their master for most of their life so that they can absorb the chi passed on to them from their master. I hope this will give a clear idea why energy training is always passed on from one master to another.

I strongly believe that it should not be that ways nowadays as if people are taught properly and in a open way with no secrets then it can benefit everyone.

Flowers in nature only bloom when the time is right.

LEVEL 2 (CONNECTING ONESELF WITH NATURE)

Nature is the source of all Energy, once you have connected within yourself you will be able to connect and receive nature's energy to further strengthen your body and organs.

In Chinese Philosophy everything in Nature is made up of five elements:

METAL - WOOD - WATER - FIRE - EARTH

These elements are all around us, however the ancient Chinese energy Masters believed that the energy from these elements are primarily present in the air which we breathe. When harnessed and balanced they can also rejuvenate the life force of a human being and enable them to live a balanced if not longer life.

An analogy I like to use is that when you see light you do not see any colour, however as we know from physics; light consists of seven colours in the rainbow spectrum. This is how I like to think of the five elements that are present in the air.

This is why it is important not to pollute the environment - especially the air as it will disrupt the balance of energy and result in poorer health for the inhabitants of our planet, it will harm all living things.

A common misconception I find is that when people discuss or teach the five elements, they look only to the materials around them which are made of Metal, Wood, Water, Fire and Earth - yet this is not always correct as you cannot breathe in a physical object such as wood or metal and this could have bad consequences!

The material elements are the result of the energy around us and millions of years of formation of this energy into physical matter.

The five elements are linked to the five main organs of your body:

Metal is linked to the Lungs
Wood is linked to the Liver
Water is linked to the Kidneys
Fire is linked to the Heart
Earth is linked to the Stomach
Once students understand this connection with nature then they will taught how to connect with and collect nature's enegy.

LEVEL 3 (HUMAN ENERGY TAI CHI FORM)

Tai Chi is popular throughout the world and Tai Chi, practitioners are commonly seen performing relaxed movements using their hands and simple footwork.

Tai Chi originated from the Wudang mountains in China, the birthplace of Taoism. Taoism is a Chinese philopsophy which translates into English as "The Way" or "The Path". It is a philosphy explaining the unity of humans and nature and they use these principles to practise self cultivation by harmonising their actions, such as Tai chi - with the rhythms of nature in order to achieve inner peace.

What I have observed in the recent popularity of Tai Chi is that many people learn it in a commercialised form which lacks any substance and energy. Just following the movements and not understanding the concepts or feeling the energy will not further your goals of training and is cheating the practitioner of any self cultivation.

At this level students learn the Human Energy Tai Chi Form. The form is a series of movements that allows them to balance and control the energy they have accumulated through training.

A student will learn at this level that softness always overcomes the hard and the highest level of Human Energy is to be like water. Even though water is soft, yet yielding - however it can overcome whatever is rigid and hard.

LEVEL 4 (CONNECTING THE MIND)

Chi flows through channels in our body. These channels are mapped out by pressure points and are comparable to a train or subway map, the stations would be the pressure points and all the stations or points connected make up the travel route or in this case the channel for the energy to travel around your body.

At this level a student will learn energy stretching. This will open up the channels in their body and allow the chi to connect the body with the mind. Eventually with practice the mind will empty, all thoughts: negative and positive will be still. The body and mind will connect and start the body's self healing mechanism.

LEVEL 5 (TRAINING FOR THE 4 SEASONS)

At this level the student will be taught energy training in different seasons and how the changes in the seasons affect the body differently.

Autumn (Preparing for Winter):
This is the time when the weather starts to cool down, students will learn how to prepare the body, mind and soul for the coming winter.

This is important as the body will face more stress and strain than usual, due to cold weather and possible harsh conditions.

Winter (Maintaining Health):
You need to strengthen the body to withstand the cold winter and maintain good health by practising the hard chi kung techniques (practising techniques in a stronger manner).

Spring (Collecting Energy):
This is the season when all things come alive and is also the time with the highest yang (positive) energy. This is the time to collect, harness and cultivate in order to strengthen the body mind and soul.

Summer (Cooling the Body):
The weather has reached it's peak and it can be too hot, so it is important to practise the soft energy exercises such as the soft tai chi form to cool the body down.

LEVEL 6 (CONNECTING THE SOUL)

Sound is connected to our soul, if a student has practised diligently and has successfully connected their body and mind then they can connect their soul. At this level a student will start to be able to project their energy.

A student will learn and practise the five following sounds:

1. Ha (Enables the lungs to receive more oxygen)
2. He (This sound releases the toxins from the liver)
3. Chu (Strengthens the kidney and it's functions)
4. Chee (Maintains a consistent heartbeat)
5. Eeee (Improves digestion in stomach and intestines)

LEVEL 7 (ACHIEVING "HEALING HANDS")

Students now able to project their energy will begin to channel it into their palms which can be used to relieve minor health issues such as: headaches, strains and physical stress.

LEVEL 8 (CERTIFICATION)

Students will receive their Human Energy Instructor Certification after they have revised and perfected all which they have learnt in level one to seven.

They will be able to instruct others in this energy programme to pass on this knowledge and skills to the next generation and the generation after.

After a student has completed all levels the energy training is continued through:

1. Proper food and diet
2. Energy breathing
3. Energy exercises to strengthen the immune system
4 . Making sure the body stays healthy practising the energy exercises at least ten minutes a day
5. Meditating in order to calm the body to boost the immune system

CONVERSATION WITH MY MASTER

One evening after training as usual we went to have dinner then tea to discuss the finer points of training. What had been bothering me for quite sometime is that how come a strong and healthy person who even practised martial arts and chi kung could suddenly suffer from heart failure or even cancer and other health issues. To me that does not make sense and is not logical. This is not what training martial arts is all about, it is about maintaining a long and disease free life to the end. As I had started training in chi kung with him I did understand some of its principles - like connecting heaven and earth and the five elements. I was not very clear about the rest and the reason why we need to do all these other things first. What he told me fascinated me and it opened my mind to a new world and thinking in my life. Writing this book has given me an opportunity to share this with you.

This philosophy and thinking has been with us for centuries, yet few have discovered it until now. What I like to ask is are we going in the right direction?, and have we forgotten the basic fundamentals of human existence. He told me that we humans are completely different from all others living things on earth. The day we are born we are helpless and weak and we need to be taken care of.

When we are conceived in the womb it takes us nine months and then we are born. So what does this have to do with energy training? He said that it is important to know the beginning of life. As the baby grows in the womb the mothers body will nourish it and feed it until the baby is ready to be born.

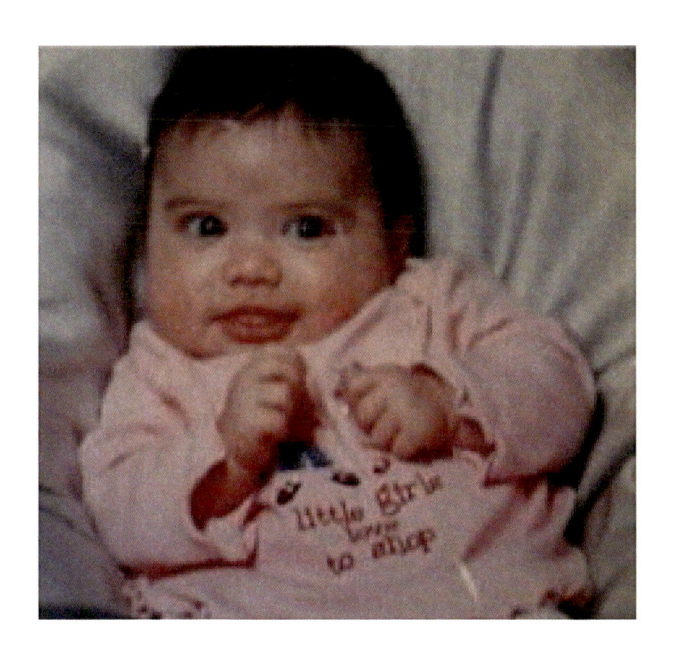

NEW BORN HAS 100 PERCENT "CHI"

But even after nine months, the baby is still not ready to be born, in other word he is born prematurely making him helpless and weak. How could that be? The mother's nourishing energy has been used up and will not be able to continue supporting the baby inside her womb, therefore the baby has to leave the womb before it is ready. The size of the baby's head is not fully developed and is bigger than the mother pelvis and that is why human childbirth can be so hard when compared to animals.

Nevertheless once the baby is born he will have 100% chi or life force in him and when he takes his first breath on earth that is the beginning of his life on earth. Every living thing is greatly influence by energy, human energy and nature energy and it give us life.
The parents will protect and look after him or her until they are ready to look after themselves.

Just like the way in the journey of energy and martial arts that one chooses to embark on. The master will guide and teach his philosophy and knowledge to him just like his master before. By practising and harnessing his chi, the student's chi will mature and be strong enough to sustain him for the rest of his life that is why it takes such a long time to reach master level.

But people nowadays have changed and lost all the basic understanding of human existence on earth. If a student learns and leaves before accomplishing the proper level not only is he wasting the masters time and energy but it will harm his own body too, therefore energy training must be taught gradually and is not an art that can be commercialised.

That was quite a lesson to me, the deep thinking and wisdom of thousands of years ago; hearing this I wanted more of this amazing training wisdom passed down from master to student.

CHAPTER 21

Healing Experiences

HEALING EXPERIENCE, CANCER PATIENT

It was in 1988, after nearly sixteen years, that I was fully authorised by my Master to use my energy healing ability to help the sick and weak and even cancer sufferers. I was thankful and happy that I had reached that high level but thinking back I did suffer a setback of how sick I had became when I attempted to help a cancer sufferer before. My master had decided to emigrate to Canada so in my mind was, if I fell sick, who would I turn to?

I asked him should I do my healing and also should I charge people? He said in modern times people live in a different era and time, we do need money to pay our bills and put food on the table for our family so taking money for our work is acceptable. Having said that, how can one measure life force and its worth?

He said treat it by half an hour sessions and charge the patient a fee for that time. It's hard to explain to them what you do with your energy - most people have lost this sort of feeling and understanding and have resorted to science taking drug. They do not necessarily understand what energy healing is, so it is best to do my best and let them judge.

No one can measure what life force is and its value. When one is giving energy healing to others, the body, mind and soul are connected sending all your life force to help and heal that person. It's like a mother giving her unconditional love to her child with no question asked. That is why true energy masters usually only send their hard earned life force to their loved ones.

It is not a business or something to be commercialised. He also told me if I decided to do healing then I should also carry out good deeds like working in charity centres to help the old and sick as a volunteer so that it will balance the circle of Tao.

My third real experience with a cancer patient was my student who used to train in Tai Chi and Human Energy with me. She was a wife of a diplomat in London and was very much interested in my energy teaching, but after two years she had to move to another part of London. Also because of her husband's work she was always busy looking after him and the training time was therefore not suitable, so I told her maybe there were other Tai Chi teachers near her area so she still could train.

I had not heard from her for nearly one and a half years. One morning around 11am I received a phone call in my shop and on the other end it was her. I was surprised and happy to hear from an old student. She told me that she was calling to say goodbye to me. So I asked her if she was leaving London and going back to her country. I knew that her husband's work took them travelling to work in different countries.

She said no, the reason she called me was that to say her final goodbye. I was puzzled - what does that mean? I asked her again. She told me that she had womb cancer stage 4, and shared with me her family history and that her grandmother and mother had all died of womb cancer at the age of 48 — the same age as she was now.

She also said that they had removed her womb and that she might have three to six months to live and to take up chemotherapy treatment after two weeks. I told her that her body would not be strong enough to go through the chemo treatment and if she did, it would be likely that her time here would lessen. I asked her to come to my shop so that I could help her with my energy.

She said that she is in so much pain they had given her the strongest pain killer and even morphine to no avail and it fell like a million needles sticking in her stomach - she said she would rather die now than live. I said please try to come to me, that maybe her husband could bring her, or I could go to her.

She said that he is busy working and in meetings, so generally she is on her own at home and that besides he did not believe in energy healing 'stuff' and that he would not agree to it, as the most advanced medicine cannot do anything to help what could I do. In my thoughts I considered what kind of a man doesn't at least give his wife a chance to see if I can help her - nothing is guaranteed not even good medicine and operations.

Eventually I could only say that it was her decision and I wished her the best of luck. I did not hear from her for three days. On the fourth day a black cab stopped in front of my shop; when the door of the cab opened it was her struggling to get out. Luckily I had three students in the shop and immediately I told them to help her out of the cab. It was a struggle as she was quite a big lady at nearly six foot tall and obviously very ill.

Finally we managed to sit her down. I always remember the first words she said were "Please, whatever you do Sifu, don't touch my stomach", and then she added, "I am not sure what I am doing here, I woke up this morning and the pain was so bad I couldn't sleep, eat, talk or walk - someone up there must have told me to come to you."

I told her to relax and I will reduce the pain from her first to make her more comfortable. She look at me in a doubtful way and again asked not to even think of touching her stomach - I said not to worry; I told her to relax and close her eyes.

I placed my left palm on top of her stomach, six inches away without touching her, and then sent healing energy into her stomach to reduce the swelling and blockages that caused the pain. I saw on her face she was instantly more relaxed and calmer. After twenty minutes I placed my palm on her stomach, this time there were no warnings from her and it did not give her pain. After an hour, most of her pain had gone.

All my students were amazed, they had never witnessed my healing power until now and yet they still cannot believe it. When she opened her eyes she said that she had the most incredible feeling as though she had an outer body experience, she felt that the pain just floated out of her body and she felt warm and tingly all over her body, as though it was coming alive.

There was no more pain and she cried with joy. I told her to rest and let the chi continue to heal her body. I also told her if she did undergo chemo treatment that she must come to me so that I can send my chi to protect all her organs. With that advice she walked out of my shop on her own and with no pain.

She had ten chemo treatments and each time she came to me to receive my energy healing. There was no hair loss or any bad side effects and she was given the all clear from her doctor after a year. The medical staff were puzzled by her recovery and told her it was nothing short of a miracle that she survived.

Since her recovery I asked her about her experiences with the other tai chi master. She said that during her training in chi kung, the master told the students to punch each other in the stomach to increase their chi power in the Tan Tien (life force area).

I was shocked and horrified - how could that be, hitting a woman in the stomach does not strengthen her, it actually harms her womb and stomach.

I asked her - was it after being punched in the stomach area that she got bad pains and bleeding followed. She said yes. I asked her for this so called master's name - so that I could go and tell him what I thought about his teaching.

She knew that from her experience with me that I don't tolerate bad teachers, because not only had it ruined her health but in this case it nearly killed her.

She dared not tell me who he was but when I asked around I knew who he was, so one evening I went to his school and stood in front of him and told his students what he had done and challenged him: if he could defeat me I would leave him alone.

If not, he should not teach *his* so called "tai chi". He refused to fight with me and instead called the police. They came and gave me a warning. I later found out that he had left the school and was teaching somewhere else. I hope he got the message from me.

At one time I was in Munich, Germany where I had several patients, some with cancer and some with other illnesses. It had been a long day, starting at 9am and finishing around 11pm. When I arrived back at my hotel, my friend asked me if it was possible for me to go to see one last patient, a lady who was a retired doctor and had had a very bad problem with her stomach for over fifteen years.

She and her husband were both top doctors and had tried everything to help her but had not been successful. My friend told me that initially they wanted to book an appointment with me but her husband was very sceptical about letting her see me - so had previously decided not to. That evening the pain was so bad that she asked if I could go and help her. Even though I was tired I decided to help her with my healing.

When I arrived at their house the husband opened the door and the first thing he said was if I was "the so called witch doctor" who thought that I could help his wife, when all the advanced medicines and treatments couldn't do it. I looked at him, but I kept my cool and stayed focused on why I was there. When I met her she was lying on the sofa holding her stomach and saying that the pain was unbearable.

Her stomach was so swollen with lots of blockages and full of gas. I explained to her that her stomach was so "ying" that it needed some "yang" energy - she looked at me with confusion, not understanding what I was saying. I told her not to worry and placed my palms on her stomach. She felt the heat from my palm and after 20 minutes the swelling had subsided and the pain had lessened, she was relieved and very surprised to feel so much better. I told her to rest, drink plenty of warm drinks like tea and to not eat cheese, dairy products or shellfish like mussels and prawns for at least three months, she nodded with approval so I left.

After two months had passed I went back to see more patients and this time she was the first on the list. I thought that she probably wanted to boost her energy so I went to see her again. Upon arrival her husband opened the door but this time he was not so rude.

She was lying on the bed and complaining again about the pain in her stomach. I asked her how long it had been like this and she said it started two weeks ago. After further questioning I discovered that she had eaten cheese which she felt was good for her. I told her that her stomach was still not strong enough to digest those types of food.

I had previously warned her about eating cheese and that this was probably the cause of the problem. I said I would do it for her this time but if she did not listen to my advice I could not come again as it was waste of my energy healing and time, despite being paid. She agreed and since then she has told me that she feel great so good and thanked me for my healing.

A HOPEFUL WIFE

A couple who wanted to conceive visited me. It was one afternoon when I had a visit from them - the wife wanted to receive some healing from me. But the experience took me aback concerning people, relationships and their perspective of money.

The woman told me that they had been trying to have a baby but each time, two months after she got pregnant, she lost it through miscarriage. They had three IVF treatments and it cost them a fortune but they were desperate to have a baby as she was approaching her fortieth birthday, she felt that it might be too late if it didn't happen then. I explained to them that her womb was not strong enough to hold on to the foetus; it's like building a castle on sand, the foundation is not strong enough and eventually it will collapse. So they could try as much as they liked - but it would not work. The only way would be to strengthen her womb first, then clear the blockages so the eggs could flow down easily to be fertilised by the sperm. I also asked if her husband's sperm count was healthy. They said yes so I told her the problem was her weakened womb.

In order to help her I would be that I can send my energy to the stomach and womb area to strengthen it and release the blockage and rid any pain or swelling around it. Her husband asked me how much would that cost. I told him that it would be fifty pounds for half an hour and she would have to come for one more treatment. He looked at me with disgust and said it was too expensive, it might not even work, is there any guarantee. I looked at him smiling and asked how much did he pay for his IVF, he said loudly: "thousands" and I replied was there any guarantee?

He just kept quiet and said that he would not want to pay that fee and offered me twenty pound. I told him that I didn't need his money and asked them to go. His wife was upset and embarrassed - but she had to go with him. I was thinking how could he behave like this? Does he not care about his wife's feelings and opinion?

After a week I saw her standing in front of my shop so I went out to greet her. She apologised for her husband's behaviour. I told her not to worry and that I get it all the time! She told me that they were running out of money for the IVF treatments and as I looked at her face I could see she was sad and desperate. I told her to come into my shop and asked her if she wanted some healing from me and she said that she could only afford fifty pounds but needed the recommended two treatments from me. I told her not to worry I would do it for her. When she heard that her face lit up as though she really believed that I could help her. That expression made me feel good as she came to me not just as a client but as someone who truly believed and trusted me.

I did two sessions for her and after that I did not see her for nearly nine months. One morning I saw a heavily pregnant lady standing in front of my shop. When I went to see who she was I realised it was the lady who came to me for healing! She greeted me with a big smile and said that she wanted to make sure she could carry the baby for at least eight months before coming to see me. I congratulated her and wished her the best. When she had her baby she called me and thanked me for my help.

It was a beautiful girl. I felt good when I heard the news; the feeling of changing people lives with my energy, something that no money or material things can replace. To me it's only a job and I am always prepared to get criticised - maybe I have grown up and have more tolerance and patience with people.

Therefore it is important to listen and take heed of my advice — through all the years of my healing experience I have discovered many things and am able to realise the issues early on.

CHAPTER 22

Success and Failure in Healing

SUCCESS AND FAILURE IN HEALING

I have had many successes in my energy healing over the years but I have also come across some difficult cases when it was too late to help them, by the time they asked for my help they had left it too late.

Energy healing is not just someone placing his palms on the patient and expecting the patient to feel better. The person who does the healing must have at least twenty years of training under a true master. Also the patient must not leave it too late. In that case no advanced medicine or energy healing can help. As I always say, prevention is better than cure.

In one case I was asked to help a lady who had stage 4 womb cancer and was also bleeding, by one of my former patients who had received my energy healing and had recovered from her illness.

I agreed to see her and as she lived in the north of England in Lancashire, I made an appointment to meet her and see whether or not I would be able to help her. She told me she was in great pain and still bleeding, the doctor wanted to operate on her followed by chemotherapy

She was also being given strong doses of morphine which made her more tired and was even reducing her appetite. When I arrived the first thing I did was to try to stop the bleeding. After two hours of energy healing on her stomach, the pain had subsided and the bleeding had also been considerably reduced. I rested for half an hour, had something to eat and drink, and then continued. The next phase was to reduce the pain and swelling further and then stop the bleeding.

I carried on with my healing hands on her stomach for another 45 minutes, then rested for 15 minutes, and made myself a hot drink to recharge my energy for another 45 minutes of healing.

After nearly five hours of my healing most of her pain was greatly reduced and the bleeding had nearly stopped. I told her to rest, drink plenty of warm drinks like hot water with slices of fresh ginger. This would boost her red blood cells and I told her I needed to see her again. Hopefully after she had my first healing session the bleeding would stop completely, the pain would reduce and the cancer cells would shrink.

She went to her doctor five days after my healing and I was told her stomach swelling had been reduced greatly and the bleeding had stopped completely!

She now needed no operation but she had to go for chemotherapy - to which she agreed. I told her that if she did the chemotherapy she would need me to carry on sending my healing energy into her body to protect the other organs, as her body was still in need of energy to protect it. I decided to call her, and I even emailed her four times telling her she was playing a dangerous game. In my mind I wondered was it that she did not want to spend money on the healing or did she not believe in me? She never answered my calls.

So I got in contact with one of her friends and she told me that she had had four chemotherapy sessions and apparently the cancer cells had shrunk considerably. I told her friend that was good news, but if she still did not contact me to have more energy healing to protect her organs, the cancer would strike again and this time it could be fatal. I told her friend to tell her that she must see me so that I could help to stop that happening.

Unfortunately she did not even bother to contact me or answer my calls. After one month her friend called me and told me she had passed away, because as I had predicted, the cancer cells had spread to most of the organs and this time it was fatal.
I was saddened to hear this, and truly upset, but as I sat in the park meditating in order to connect with nature to calm myself down I remembered what my Master said to me.

I am here to help and send them my message, if they don't listen then they are playing Russian roulette with their life. Whether or not they believe what I say is not important.

In the end the decision to live or not is theirs. I felt much better and moved on to my next cancer patient.
There were others who took powerful drugs for it, but unfortunately it was too much for the heart to take.

At the end of the day - they themselves have to look after their health, no one can help them if they don't want to be helped. I am only a messenger, my job is to send them my message.

Nevertheless most people who follow my advice and energy healing have a high recovery rate. I wish that those who don't listen to me would start to, then I think my success rate would be even higher.

People take life for granted, if you do not learn to take care of your health then you will not enjoy a long life.

Life is precious.

CONNECTING WITH NATURE

CHAPTER 23

Human Energy Experiment

EXPERIMENT WITH HUMAN ENERGY 2010

It was July the 8th, I was invited to Geneva by Monsieur Pier Rubesa who has a machine that can measure sound and how it is affected by energy.the effect of energy healing and the energy field of a human.

He calls it a ,"bio harmonic" machine, which measures the effect of energy or chi that relates to the biological function of a human.
A sensor is connected to the finger of the patient, which can measure the energy field before and after the healing by touch, sound, and energy healing.

Information received before, during and after healing is captured by the sensor on the patient and is transferred to the computer and analysed.

By doing this we can look at the characteristics of the field and we can then determine whether the treatment is effective or not.
This will give possibilities to people who work in energy, a way to see the effect of their work and to be able to measure the effect of their treatment in the individual.

There is a dynamic and structural energy field round the body, when a person is ill his energy field becomes unstructured and chaotic. When a person is healthy the energy field is regular and solid.

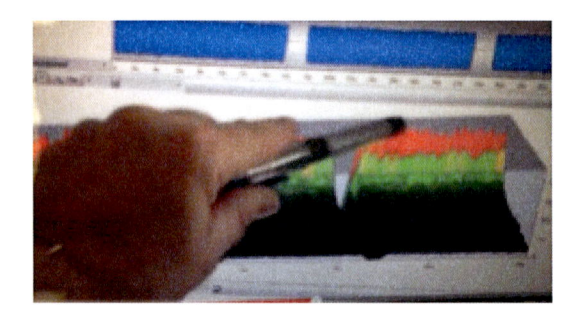

RESULTS OF EXPERIMENT

BEFORE ENERGY TREATMENT

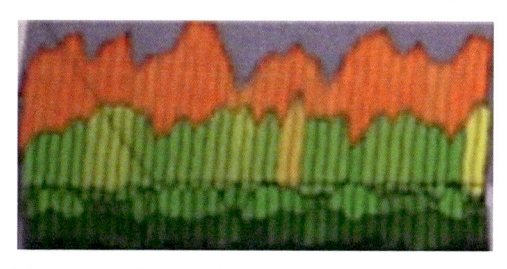

The energy field round the body is barely visible, in other word: the energy field surrounding his body is unstable due to his illness.

DURING ENERGY HEALING

The energy field or life force is starting to rejuvenate.

AFTER ENERGY HEALING

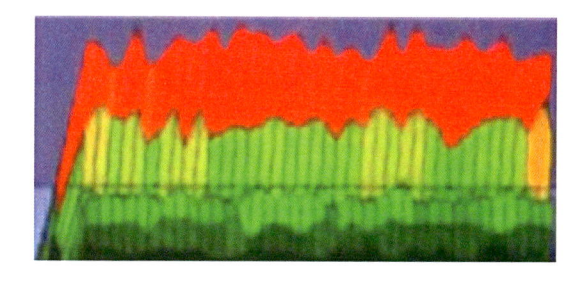

The energy field in the body is strengthened.

DENSITY OF ELECTRICAL FIELDS

BEFORE ENERGY TREATMENT

There was absolutely no density at the 40000-48000 hz frequency level.

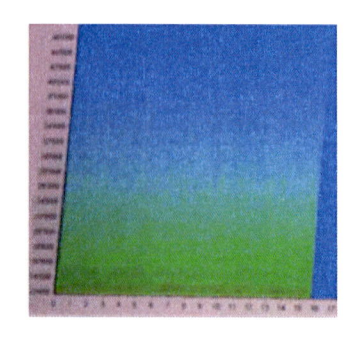

DURING ENERGY TREATMENT

The density is now increased

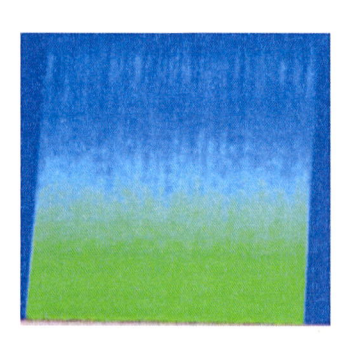

AFTER ENERGY TREATMENT

This density now remains inside the body, the electrical field of the body has been restructured and strengthened.

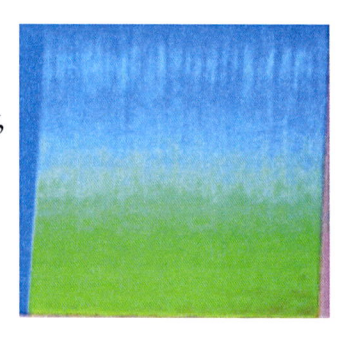

MY OPINION ON MEASURING HUMAN ENERGY

At first I was reluctant to do the experiment, as in my opinion, energy healing does not require scientific proof. However, on second thoughts, people nowadays rely heavily on measureable facts and figures, so I decided to go ahead with it. To a lot of skeptics this might not be proof that energy healing does work, I believe that everyone is entitled to their opinion. I firmly believe if one learns energy healing from a true master and practises properly then this form of healing will be effective.

Facts and figures which most people look for nowadays are good but not everything that the machine or computer tells us is accurate. We have feelings and emotions which can never be measured, yet no-one can deny their existence. Energy healing has been with us for thousands of years and has been proven successful by many great masters in the past healing the sick and weak. So do we need modern technology to judge it? Most modern medicines are tested on animals, I strongly disagree with this. We are humans, not rats or guinea pigs. No doubt they say that rats possess DNA like humans but we are not rats. There might be some similarity in DNA but we are human.

For example the drug Thalidomide was tested on animals and considered safe to be given to pregnant women. If science has advanced so far, why can't we find a humane method of testing drugs? The world is changing all the time but we are still human beings, we cannot carry on consuming like this, raping Mother Earth, destroying forests and nature to produce more drugs. This has to stop - if we don't, then it will be catastrophic. In the last few years we have already seen a vast reduction in the bird and bee populations, and more and more species are on the brink of extinction.

I strongly believe there will be a great impact on our future generations, from all this careless destruction, motivated by greed.

We are all children of Mother Earth, we need to show her some respect. We all need to take responsibility for maintaining our own good health, and this begins with a balanced lifestyle, including proper nutrition and an understanding of the principles of human energy.

SWOLLEN, BRUISED AND BLEEDING KNEE FROM FALL BEFORE HUMAN ENERGY TREATMENT

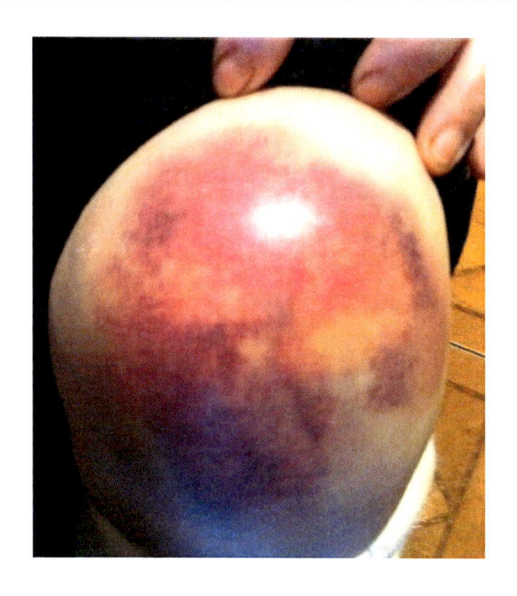

AFTER 25 MINUTES OF HUMAN ENERGY TREATMENT, LEG COULD NOW BE EXTENDED

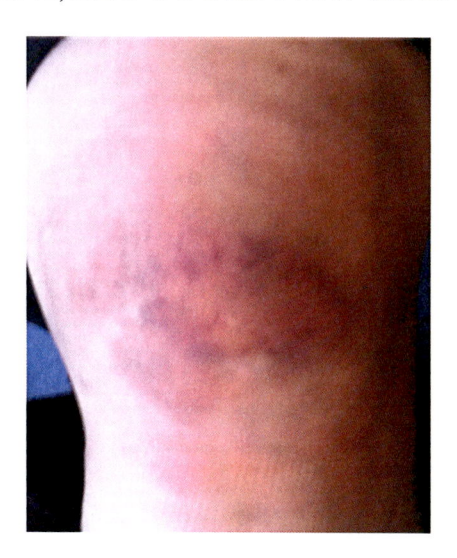

CHAPTER 24

Some Testimonials

TESTIMONIALS

Here are a few of testimonials from a handful of patients, I am happy to share some of these wonderful experiences with you.

People who have received healing from me often share their experiences. For many it can mean a major change to their health and life and they are keen to share this so that others may benefit. Receiving healing is often an unusual experience for people, unlike any other form of healing, and the results can be quite startling. I have provided a selection of people's experiences below, but if you would like further information by all means contact me directly to ask questions or address any concerns.

WOMB CANCER — GIVEN 3 MONTHS TO LIVE

"Had womb cancer and was given three months to live. The numerous chemotherapy sessions and operations had left me in unbearable pain. While bidding my friends my last goodbye, I recalled my Tai Chi classes with Master Austin Goh. With great excruciating pain, I had to be assisted by four people from the taxi to his shop. From his healing hands, after about 15 minutes, I felt relief from my pain and an hour later my pain had disappeared. Thereon, after each chemotherapy session, I stopped losing my hair and had no more side effects. Thank you to a true master and the angels that sent him."

Holle Brant, Munich.

TERMINAL CANCER — OPERATION NOT NEEDED, HOPE RESTORED

"I was diagnosed with terminal bowel cancer with metastases to liver and told I would need an operation to shut down my bowel. I was in a state of shock when a friend suggested I see Austin Goh — I had never heard of him but since having 2 sessions with him I no longer need an operation. The oncologist has also decided to treat me with a course of chemo. Although no promises have been made the situation is much improved from when I initially spoke to my surgeon who said there was nothing to be done to help me."

Victoria K, Lincoln

TERMINAL BREAST AND WOMB CANCER — GIVEN THE ALL CLEAR

"After having gone through six operations for breast and womb cancer, I was feeling weak and in atrocious pain, with doctors not being able to do anything more for me. I flew to London for a month's treatment with Master Austin Goh, whom I had met once before. On my return, at my regular check up, I was given the all clear. It was the happiest day for me and my family, thanking Buddha for sending him to me."

Nancy Ng, 68, Hong Kong

BREAST LUMP IS NOW REDUCING IN SIZE

"Greetings Austin, Thank you very much for the healing and the support you have given to me it has been really beneficial. My breast lump is now reducing in size and I am so grateful to you for your time and especially your healing power. Love and respect."

Sharon, London

LONG TERM NECK PAIN RELIEVED

"I met Austin for the first time in October 2009. He treated my neck for an old whiplash injury that I had suffered in March 2001. During the second 30-minute treatment he managed to unblock my stiff neck and gently replace the vertebra that had been out of place for 8 years. As a consequence my back and my neck feel a lot better. What a dozen physiotherapy sessions could not manage to relieve, Austin managed to solve in less than an hour with his healing hands."

Susanna, Geneva

LONG-TERM ARTHRITIS PAIN AND HEART PROBLEMS

"I arranged for Austin Goh to see a good friend of mine for her long term arthritis pain and heart problems. She had been in unrelenting pain for a number of years despite many treatments and was now unable to walk more than a few steps and was spending most days in bed. After one session with Austin she said she felt ten years younger and had so much energy she could not believe it. Her pain was almost totally gone and the next day she was able to go down the steps into her garden and walk to the shops. I have never heard her so happy. She said it was the best present she had ever had." -

Louise Harley, London

SERIOUS INFECTION AND FOOD ALLERGIES ELIMINATED

"When I spoke to Austin Goh I had just been to hospital and had a terrible experience being questioned and examined by six different doctors and surgeons over a three day period, with endless blood tests and scans, whilst they tried to figure out what was wrong with me. Although they meant well the excruciating pain and whole hospital experience was so physically and mentally draining I felt worse than ever-and I hit a new low. This was the latest in a very long line of every increasing health issues. I had had years of digestive problems and over time had become intolerant to most food, suffering terrible pain, very low energy, and I had slowly gained more and more weight as my body seemed to cope less and less.

I couldn't remember a time where I wasn't ill; pain had become normal. Over the years I been told I had IBS, food allergies, viruses, stomach ulcers, appendicitis, suspicions of worse — I was tired of

tests, possible diagnoses and trying what felt like a million different medications and treatments, none of which worked. After three days they told me I had a serious infection in my abdomen
(similar to a cyst) and that I would need an operation to remove it.

They wanted to perform the operation the following week but luckily I said I would prefer to have it later. When Austin Goh said he could help in my mind I thought "ok one more thing I will try but this is it — after this no more, I am just going to accept that this is my existence".

Austin gave me healing over three sessions; even by the end of the first session I could feel a massive change in the way my body was working. By the end of three, my infection had gone, my swollen stomach was flat (I hadn't even realized it had been swollen. I felt lighter, younger and energized for the first time in over ten years.

And the surgeon gave me the all clear with no operation needed. I couldn't believe it — years of pain gone! I could eat any food I wanted again and was able to exercise and lose weight easily.

It was the first time as an adult I had truly felt healthy — it is hard to say in words how much that meant to me and still does. It dramatically changed my life and I now have the energy to make new life choices. After spending so much time, money and stress on conventional western options with no results, I would recommend anyone with health issues to see Austin — he is a truly amazing man, a very rare find in this day and age. In fact I would suggest he should be your first point of call and not your last."

Rose, England

INABILITY TO DIGEST

"I had treatment for Hepatitis C for a year. After that I felt really ill for a long time, and my stomach kept growing even if the only thing I ate was porridge. When I ate, it felt as if all the food was stuck in my throat and that happened even when I drank tea or other fluids.

I went to see Master Austin Goh and the results of the first treatment exceeded all my expectations as my stomach went down by at least 5cm, and I felt light, like I was absolutely healthy! After that treatment the food started to digest properly. I could feel a clear difference. The amazing thing was that the effects of the treatment lasted for 3-4 months.

After that I went for another treatment and felt great after it. I haven't been back since as I am digesting food properly and I can look after myself with the advice that Master Austin gave me. I greatly appreciate Master Goh's help and strongly recommend him as a talented professional in his field."

Tamara Jegorova, Latvia.

PERSISTENT COUGHING

"I met Master Goh for the first time when I was going to join his human energy class in London Chinatown. It was full of elderly in the class and was packed with students. I was so lucky they accepted me because Master Goh allowed me to join the class. ...The training was great, it was easy and I felt like 20 years younger after the class, it was unbelievable the way he conducted his class with so much laughter and enjoyment. I had never been to such a class before even though I have had Tai Chi and Chi Kung training with various master in Hong Kong and London. What amazes me is that he teaches the class for free just to help the elderly . We are so lucky.

My testimony is in reference to my grandson of 13 months; who was suffering with a high temperature and coughing without stopping for quite sometime and doctor's medicine was not working.
With this in mind I took my grandson to Master Goh to ask whether he can help. The first thing he said that my grandson had a very high temperature and that it was coming from the heart and lungs . Without saying anything he just placed
his palm on his heart and to my surprise my grandson let him. Ten minutes later Master Goh told me that he had brought the temperature down and he should feel better and the cough should stop soon.

 I was taken aback, no way, I then placed my palm on my grandson's forehead and the fever and temperature had gone.
Master Goh then said he should sleep well in the night and he will be back to normal the next morning. That night my grandson stayed with me and he slept well; like a lord and the next morning he smiling laughing and was back to normal. All my life I had met some amazing healers or chi master but he blew me away Thank you master Goh for teaching me and looking over my

family too. Words cannot describe your incredible healing".

Fong, Age 62. Hong Kong

BROKEN ARM

"It was last year that I had an accident at home while doing some house work. I slipped and fell to the floor of my kitchen as I landed I placed my palm on the ground to soften the fall. Unfortunately my arm gave way and I broke it into 2. The pain was excruciating and I was rushed to emergency ward. After taking lots of painkillers, the arm was finally set together in a cast but the pain was so excruciating that I could not sleep or eat for few days.

Seeing this my wife suggested for me to see master Austin Goh, I couldn't fathom what he could do to help me. Reluctantly I went with my wife to see Master Goh. When I saw him for the first time I was so surprised he looked like a young 35 year old man let alone being a master of healing and martial arts. The first thing he said was that he will reduce the pain in the first 5 minutes. In my mind I was sure that this young looking guy was a bit mad, no way would this happen.

The moment he placed his hand on my palm I could feel a warmness inside my palm and moving towards my arm area, it was a great feeling and the pain in my broken bones just melted away slowly, it was awonderful and amazing feeling. I was able to breathe better and the movements in my fingers are much more flexible and loose, there was no pain when I moved it.
 It was the best feeling of my life and when I went to the hospital to have my cast removed the doctor said the break had healed and it was unbelievable that it had healed.
I was discharge with no further appointments. How he did it still

confuses me, all science I knew as a logical man went out of the window; whatever it is I am so grateful to him. Thank You Master Austin Goh"

Mr. Chow, Age 73, London

OPERATION RECOVERY

"My name is Ken and I am 71 years old. For nearly four years I have been attending Austin Goh's Human Energy Class and would like to briefly tell you how they have helped me recover from two very serious conditions. The exercises we have been taught are easy, anyone at any age could do them, however, they are powerful and effect healing.

Eighteen months ago I had an infection that settled on the heart and aortic valve. The cause of this was a bowel cancer - so it was necessary to have surgery to remove the tumor. I was very pleased to learn to hear that the cancer had all gone, so the first part of my recovery began. All through this illness I practiced my exercises with Austin's advice, advocating that they should be done gently as they were just as effective. Six months later I have had to have the aortic valve replaced. This operation was judged to be difficult and risky. Right up to the day of the surgery I continued to do my exercises, especially the breathing ones as I felt this would help me rid my body of the toxins of anaesthetic.

The valve was replaced, eventually, using a keyhole technique (TAVI) and I was told that I would be in intensive care for at least 24 hours. Even in the Intensive Care Ward I gently shook my hands in the way we have been taught - to keep my blood flowing. Within a few hours it was deemed that my recovery was so good I could return to a ward - so no overnight stay in the ICU.

After a check up 4 weeks later the Cardiologist wrote in a letter to the GP that "this patient has had a remarkable recovery" - I do not have to be checked again now for another year. I firmly believe that following Austin Goh's program of Human Energy and the healing energy we exchange in the class, I have healed in far less time than would be normal for a man my age I feel so well and would recommend Austin's program to anyone - you do not have to be ill to feel the benefit of health and energy. It is an amazing experience."

Ken, Eastbourne

CHAPTER 25

Things I tried but failed

THINGS I TRIED BUT FAILED

NUNCHAKU SHOWING OFF

Bruce Lee was an inspiration to a lot of people, especially to me as I am proud that he was my kung fu uncle. Everyone wanted to be like him, including me; the whole world went nunchaku mad. I was quite good with it and one evening at a party I was trying to impress some ladies so I was showing off my skills in front of them. I was doing ok so I went further by trying to spin the nunchaku round my groin to show off... I missed a catch and it hit my groin area, it was so painful I nearly turned blue, but I insisted I was ok. Never again would I try that stunt.

THINKING I COULD WALK ON WATER

After I was successful in practising my light kung fu standing on eggs without breaking them, I was so confident that I was going to learn to walk on water. I had read that there were masters in China years ago who had the ability to glide on the surface of water from one end to another on a piece of wood. This give me an idea - I should try it on a lake. I went to Hyde Park lake to try to practise on it. I found a quiet spot where there was no one around, to try my stunt.

Firstly I placed a plank on the water, I did my light breathing chi kung exercises, then slowly I tried to stand on top of the plank without sinking it. Guess what happened- it did- and I went down like a rock. When I surfaced I was met by the guard asking me what I was doing swimming in the lake. I made my excuses and left. It was a disaster stunt. As I was drying myself off, I was laughing to myself, had I gone mad?

WRESTLING A BULL TO THE GROUND

When I was in Japan I knew of a great karate master called Oyama. So I went to pay my respects; it was said that he had punched a bull's head with his bare hand, so when I arrived back in London I went to the outskirts, to a farm, and looked for a bull.

My intention was not to punch the bull's skull, but to try to wrestle the bull to bring him to the ground. Eventually I found one and quick as a flash I jumped on top of him grabbing him by the horns, he was so strong he just threw me to the ground- as I fell down I heard the farmer shouting at me what was I doing trespassing… luckily I was ok and I ran off as fast as I could.

BREAKING AN IRON BAR WITH MY ARM

One day I took a solid iron bar and tried to break it with my arm; thinking with my chi and my hard bones I should be able to break it into two.

So I took a deep breath and with all my strength I smashed my arm onto the iron bar; once my arm reached it I felt the pain in my arm as though it was going to break.

It was so painful that as I sat on the floor tears came out of my eyes. I told myself never again. The iron bar was still in one piece.

TRYING TO BE A DISCO DANCING KING

During the 70's the movie Saturday Night Fever was a big hit and there were disco dancing competitions everywhere, especially in the famous Empire Ballroom in Leicester Square.

As a young lad I used to go there to show off my dancing skills but unfortunately for me there were many great dancers there against whom I didn't think I stood a chance, but nevertheless, as usual, with my never say die attitude, I decided to try.

On that evening I prepared myself, put on my white suit like in the movie, and my leather pointed dancing shoes. Gelled my hair, thinking that I was looking so cool.
The trousers were tight on the top but flared out to the bottom, we called them bell bottoms.

When I arrived, there were so many people there, we all took turns to dance in the middle, surrounded by the crowds clapping and cheering - my friend who was the British disco champion showed some great moves, doing the flip and somersaulting, the crowd were going wild.

I tried to copy him, and as I was trying to flip myself upwards in the middle of a dance routine, I could feel my trousers splitting and I landed on my ankle, it was painful and embarrassing but luckily it was dark, so not many people noticed it in the crowd. I rushed to the toilet and sat on the floor. My ankle was so painful. The next day I went to see my Master for some healing, telling him that I sprained it during training. My excuse for my behaviour was that I was young and brash. Thinking back I must have been out of my mind but I don't have any regrets.

MY DANCING DAYS

WANTING TO STRENGTHEN MY GROIN

When I was in Hong Kong in the 80's I heard of a master who let people kick his groin without him getting hurt, through my curiosity I went to pay him a visit and asked him could he demonstrate for me, would he allow me to kick his groin area?

He did let me kick his groin area and amazingly he absorbed my kicking power. In my mind I was thinking he must have a strong groin if I learn it I too can possess this power, wow, maybe I can be a stallion in bed. I asked him can anyone train to do this, he said yes and asked me did I want to try. Without hesitation I said yes please.

He told me firstly that I needed to strengthen my groin muscles by hanging a weight on my willy with a rope dangling the weight and swinging it forward and backward.

Eagerly I went and strapped the rope round it and tried to lift the weight off the ground; I could feel the weight was pulling it downward and it was horribly painful round that area.

My face was red with pain but the master said now try to swing it forward and backward with your hips. I tried to thrust my hips forward and backward but the pain was unbearable. I felt like my poor crown jewels were going to drop off.

After a few minutes I couldn't take any more, I let the weight drop to the ground and then released the rope. I could still feel the pain and bruises appeared. I was frightened; maybe I'd killed my little brother and it wasn't going to work again.

After that I said thank you to the master for showing me the techniques and I left. Thinking back maybe the master was trying to teach me a lesson for kicking him too hard or just showing me how tough it was training this kung fu. Nevertheless I was in pain for nearly a week. I was worried too; luckily after ten days the pain and the bruises had gone and it was back to normal. Very happy and thankful and never, never again.

CHAPTER 26

Dreams, Hopes and Wishes

MY DREAMS

When I was a boy my dreams were never about my life as it is now. I wanted to be a great badminton player which I nearly succeeded in, representing my school and states in my school days. The support that I got from my mum when I used to travel to different parts of Malaysia for competitions was great.

And again she supported me when I had to leave for Singapore to take trials to be a pilot, which was my ultimate dream, but I failed on the final day because my hearing was not sharp enough.

At that moment I felt that my world had collapsed around me and I was heartbroken that my dream just vanished without a trace. My mum came to my side and as usual gave me encouragement and support and suggested to me about going to England to further my studies.

Never in a million years did I think that I would - my life had an unexpected turn around coming to London. It must have been meant to be. My dream now is for people to embrace my Human Energy training programme, and that my students spread Wing Chun and Human Energy in a responsible and caring way. I hope that is not too much to ask.

REACH FOR YOUR DREAMS

HOPES

As I always say, life is a journey of ups and downs, no one can predict the future or what lies ahead of us. We just have to move on with our journey and make the best of it. Life is precious and we must treasure all of it, our memories are our journey of the past, everything happens for a reason. Therefore we must live life to the full.

Looking back, was there a purpose in my life? Was I born to be different? But thinking of it I am no different than any one, we are all trying to live our lives to the fullest and to enjoy our journey on this planet.

My hope is that the human race will pay more attention to Mother Earth on which we are living, look after her it with all our heart, preserve this precious planet for our next generations to come, we humans have survived and we have done this for thousands of years, while many species have become extinct over the years.

When I was born, there were around 3 billion humans, now it's around 7 billion! We will reach 9 billion in 2050 at a rate of 80 million more humans every year, it's staggering - can the earth produce enough food to sustain that many people?

I am sure we will find a solution, thinking of it. We need to find a way to balance and live in harmony with Mother Earth.

HOPES AND SMILES

WISHES

I spent my childhood in Malaysia until 1972 and later spent most of my life living in the west, nearly 40 years of my life has been in England, Europe and the United States, my home is now here in London.

I came as a poor student and managed to do all this, it was like a dream or something out of a great adventure movie. I had some good and some bad adventures. Life goes on and looking back I am blessed to be surrounded with so many good people - I thank all of them.

For the past thirty years I have travelled all over the world helping and healing people who needed my help, especially cancer sufferers and also teaching senior citizens the human energy programme and helping them to feel better in their old age, as a volunteer in different charity centres.

To see them feeling better after training or healing gives me a lot of pleasure and most of all inner peace.

My greatest wish now is to see my children grow up to be good citizens of the world and look after themselves.

CHAPTER 27

Acknowledgements

MY GREATEST THANKS

MY MOTHER CHUNG OOI MOOI

Who loved and looked after me when I was little, now she is 82 it's my turn to look after her and I am happy and honoured to do that with all my heart.

I remember when I was six years old, I fell into a drain and smashed my head, it was bleeding so much and my mum carried me all the way to the hospital and was holding my hands while the doctor stitched me up, it was so painful but my mum put her arms round me, consoling me and I felt the pain lessen.

Later she nursed me back to health. She always supported me whenever I needed help, for that I am grateful and hopefully I will make the rest of her life much happier and she can find peace within herself.

I love you with all my heart Mother.

In Tao people are born when they receive breath. Breath is their mother and spirit dwells in their breath. When children care for their mother their breath become one in harmony.

MY GRANDFATHER

My Grandfather whose stories of his life in China and his journey to Malaysia with his family, his determination, courage and willingness to protect his family with his life is a great inspiration to me.

My Grandfather always said that the toughest decision in his life was to leave China with my Grandmother, his children and with nothing material, he was heartbroken.

He would often tell me about what he lost in China where he had worked so hard to achieve his dreams all his life but it was taken away from him by the communists.

Yet after arriving from China to Malaysia he rebuilt his empire again. It took him only a few years to do.

What an amazing man - Rest in peace Granddad.

SIFU AND SIMO

Who taught me not just his amazing Wing Chun as well as Human Energy skills and knowledge but to be a better human being and for that I am truly grateful to him.

What I cannot forget when he sent his energy into my body is that feeling of warmness, calm and inner peace was just out of this world. I had travelled the world and had experience with some of the great energy masters but no one was like him, to me he was the best of the best. I am the luckiest person to have learned from him.

Sadly my master passed away in October 1991; it was the saddest day of my life.

According to Chinese tradition, as my Master's rightful successor, when he passed away I had to meditate with nature every morning, to send energy to his spirit, from 5am to 8am for ninety days. This is to help my master's spirit cross over to the other side. In life he helped and looked after me, so in spirit I returned the goodness by sending my energy to him — it's rather like looking after our parents when they are old.

I started showing and teaching the Human Energy since 2001, ten years after my master's passing as promised.

Sifu you will always be in my heart.

UNCLE CHRIS BLACKMORE

My Uncle Chris taught me about the English culture and how to be better mannered and more disciplined with myself. He was a great man and someone I truly admired; a man of great discipline.
He taught me about the basic and finer points of table etiquette - the English way. Having lived in Malaysia I only knew how to use chopsticks and spoons to eat and never had the experience of using a knife and fork.

It was hard to learn and at first I managed stuffing the food in my mouth with the fork and also the knife. I can still see the disgusted and shocked look on the face of my uncle! One day he sat me down and explained to me that one must not put the knife with food in the mouth. The knife is for cutting the food, and the fork to pick up the food and placing into the mouth.

My uncle also taught me to say "yes please" and "no thank you" and always asked to be excused from the table, or excuse yourself from the table when you have finished your meal. In my heart this is hard as where I came from we ate and left whenever we pleased. To me it was a learning experience from a man who took great pride in good manners. And so I learnt to eat properly using the cutlery and said please and thank you wherever required, something I have passed on to my children.

My uncle was a true English gentleman which one rarely finds nowadays. Unfortunately he passed away ten years ago. It was one of the saddest days of my life.

Thank you Sir.

AUNTIE CHIU

You taught me an invaluable lesson that I cannot forget - how to keep warm in bed during winter. When I arrived in England, the first place I went to was my auntie's home in the army barracks in Maidstone, it was in October and it was very cold, coming from a hot country, to me, it was unbearable. When I slept it was so cold.
My Auntie kept asking me why I was still so cold in bed when I had my jumper, socks and even my jacket on. She was confused and surprised and could not understand why, until one evening she finally came into my room and when she saw me she burst out with laughter.

She woke me up and asked me why I wasn't sleeping under the blankets and instead using the bed sheet as a cover. I replied saying I thought it was the blanket, she laughed and told me that is the bed sheet not the blanket and I needed to go under the blanket! So I did and it was nice and warm!

The next morning my cousins Lorna and Vernon were laughing at me - I took it as though nothing had happened, how was I to know, when in Malaysia I only had one sheet because it so hot and humid there! Anyway thanks again for teaching me this important lesson, I will always remember the difference between a bed sheet and a blanket. No worries, I still love you, Auntie.

On a more serious note, thank you for all your support through the years I have been in England, for the help that you continued to give me - words cannot describe how grateful I am.

I can only say thank you and big hugs, auntie.

CHAPTER 28

Thinking Back

Final Thoughts

THINKING BACK

Thinking back, the things I did in the past have all been experiences that I can say I am proud of. This is because I believed in myself and my master. I have always wanted to push my body, mind and soul to the limit as I found working outside my comfort zone both challenging and rewarding. I trained in martial arts and energy for my own personal quest for improving my self morally and spiritually; to become a better human being.

Whether I succeeded or failed, at least I can say I made a great effort trying to further my endurance and ability; pushing myself and pushing my body to the limit. I am not looking for attention, seeking fame or recognition; as long as I am still living on Mother Earth I will find new challenges. Searching for new challenges and looking for new ways and ideas to improve my martial arts and healing ability. It is with this in mind that makes my life so interesting and fruitful.

From the day I was born in Malaysia I was destined to come to the west. As a very young boy I had been involved in many street brawl situations - being hit and kicked by others, that I think maybe it was just a dress rehearsal and preparation for the challenges and hurdles that I faced and overcame when I arrived in the west.

During the early period in London, I faced racism, criticism, and was even talked down to by my fellow Chinese colleagues, yet nothing deterred me, in fact it made me more determined to excel and to believe that I could succeed and overcome any obstacles that I might encounter.

I chose to work as a bouncer and a body guard as a personal challenge to myself; maybe it was fate, part of my journey in life but I wanted to see how far I could go, not just because I am Chinese but as a man.

During my work I had been hit and ambushed many times by people who were trying to kill or cripple me and I faced several life or death situations.

They used baseball bats, bicycle chains, knives and even guns to have a go at me. My body had been subject to many attacks, my forehead had been hit by a whisky bottle and metal bars, my body, hands and feet had seen knives and all sorts of weapons several times, leaving many scars behind.

My chin and nose had been broken few times, I nearly lost my sight by someone who wanted to blind me with a knuckle duster, my knees and my shin bones are still in pain when the weather gets cold. Yet these scars I bear each tell a story, each one represents a part of my journey to where I am today.

I survived, and I continue to thrive, due to my never say die attitude and because I believed in myself. That is why I have had to train my body and mind to perfection in my fighting techniques; to develop great speed, power and mental fitness to deal with all situations; if I made a mistake my life would be in danger, so it's not a game or a hobby, it the real deal.

Those martial arts students and self-proclaimed masters out there are sometimes naive in their thinking, that once they had reached the level of Black sash they think that they can easily handle themselves in any situation.

In the kwoon or in competitions it is completely different, it is in a controlled environment where there are no real threats to their lives while sparring and free fighting, but in the street when you are confronted with someone holding a knife or gun pointing it at you, it is very different.

You probably freeze, your heart beats faster with the anxiety of not knowing what to do. People have no mercy out in the street if they wanted to rob or attack you, there are no control, no rules. They will come to you hard and strong with the intention of hurting you without any mercy or compassion - this is how bad some human beings can behave.

This generation of martial art students have gone about the art in a different and dark way - now wanting to achieve everything in such a short time and specifically focusing on the fighting aspect. All forms of respect, tradition and discipline has seemingly gone out of the window. They enjoy watching human beings beating one another in a cage and in the kwoon, there are no morals or self discipline, instead it is based on fighting and money.

How long this will go on for I wonder? Where young children are taught to maim and dislocate each other's joints, what will happen to them when they grow up. Children are innocent and there to influence positively; if we are in disorder, how can we guide our next generation. Why do they think and behave this way, if the next generation of so called martial arts students behave like this what is the future?

Some parents are as much to blame encouraging their children to do this just for glory, the adrenaline rush and cheap thrills. Not only will it harm their bodies but their minds and thinking will also be messed up. It's time for people to regain the discipline, the respect and the honour that comes with practising martial arts. The reason for learning, for being.

My students, no matter how great or they become, they should know that their experience is not the same as mine; I live and trained in a different era when the challenges and thinking was completely different, compared to nowadays.

However I hope they think that they have overtaken me in my skills and knowledge as every true master always wants their students to be better - it's like every parent who want their children to have a better life. That is how true masters should behave. What I am saying is that if you have learnt from me I hope I have changed your life in some way and helped you to better yourself.

The experience that I have over the years will not or cannot be overtaken. That is why being a master does take time, it's the experience that a student wants to learn not just the technique and skill that is why earning the wisdom from a true master is worth more than a life long training without any understandings.

A true master will show you the right path, correct your mistakes and encourage you. His aim is to want you to pass his art to you in a correct way.

Students who previously trained with me at Wing Chun School need to maintain their checks to keep their validation to teach, up to date. Even those that had received my certificate as a black sash and had my endorsement in the past need to be checked by me every year, as they may not be teaching what I had taught them to their students and therefore without the checks will not be considered as my official representatives.

I might not understand all these laws and rights in the west but I am learning and will ensure that I will take every legal action necessary so that no one can abuse my good name and reputation, which I have earned and treasured all my life.

I believe that in order to preserve quality Wing Chun and Human Energy and take it to the next generation, I have to act now.
If I don't, the title Master has no value any more. In Wing Chun today, where so many masters emerge every day, it weakens the art. It is not what Wing Chun kung fu is all about.

Human energy is based on understanding of how your body works within itself and how it connects with nature. There are no secrets like such things as taking energy from the universe or spiritual energy, instead we are surrounded with true energy on earth - the five elements are in the air and these are connected to our organs - and if we can learn how to use them then we will achieve good and long health.

To me it is important to learn to breathe properly and maintain a good circulation as shown in my level one DVD. And to practise. No human can have the ability to use his hard earned energy to heal others if he had not been practising for over 40 years and under the guidance of a true master.

It is not possible to receive energy healing through a telephone or Skype; this is absurd and another representation of poor guidance - people are trying to prey on vulnerable people who may be sick and desperate.

People do not necessarily get strokes or heart attacks just like that. It is in your system for some time, possibly due to bad lifestyle, stress, strain or diet and maybe many bad habits, resulting in an imbalance in your system causing bad circulation and creating blockages in your body and making what I call a time bomb in the body which one day could explode. It is important to maintain a good circulation to avoid these problems.

For people who feel run down or ill and yet live a healthy lifestyle, doing lots of exercises and eating healthily may still suffer. Sometimes in life, too much of goodness also create an imbalance in your body.

The secrets of a healthy life are to gain an understanding of how to balance your diet, work and importantly, rest. In modern day thinking people seems to like to complicate things like making up new terms for things, or new exercise regimes and new diseases for the human body. The body is simple, it only needs a well-balanced lifestyle, and as long as your cells are happy you will be healthy.

2500 years ago the only way to heal was through energy healing until humans sought quick and easy solutions; often looking for financial gain in giving herbs and medicine to the sick and weak and eventually the simple ways were taken over; we lost the ability of looking after ourselves, instead depending on drugs and advanced technology to help us and putting our lives and health in someone else's hands like doctors and drugs. No one can help you if you do not take responsibility for your own health.

I wish modern doctor and scientists acknowledge that humans have feeling. Don't get me wrong, what they do is great and it is right to treat the symptoms if it brings less pain, but the disease is still there. In order to cure the disease they must find the roots of the problems.

They must also understand this in order for a body to heal, it needs to work in harmony with the rest of the organs and this takes time before the healing can be complete. If you had replace someone with a new heart or kidney, the rest of the organs will also need to work with the new organ in a harmonious way.

There is no point in having a strong heart pumping lots of blood round the body if some organs are not able to handle it, this will cause an imbalance. It is like putting a plug with four rods into a plug instead of two, it will be too much for the fuse to handle and eventually blow up.

This might not sound logical to some, as for another example, it is like replacing a Ferrari engine in a Mini - it can be too powerful for the Mini to handle that it will break down. Human Energy healing coupled with modern treatment will help a patient to recover faster, putting less stress on the body and mind and avoiding lots of side effects. By speeding up the recovery process, fewer drugs will be consumed.

Drugs companies might not like what I have said but if they too want longevity in their company, they should take note that if they carried on giving more drugs to people their body and immune system will reject it eventually, and if they give more powerful drugs the heart will not be able to take it. Their drugs will have no effect.

There will be 9 billion humans soon, so there are plenty of customers, so why not tell people the truth about the long-lasting side effects that will occur while taking too many medicine and drugs.

Unfortunately it might have gone too far now. With too many people on earth depending on drugs and medicine how long can we sustain it, this continuous robbing of Mother Earth to produce more drugs? Soon there will be nothing to take when the earth become barren and bare. If we act now, together we can still have time to reverse this process.

If each and everyone just did a small part by taking care of their health, by just practising the basic Human Energy programme regularly, they will be more healthier and consume far fewer drugs, giving earth more time to recover and heal itself from all these past and present annihilation. Then our future generations will have a home on earth.

People who decide to come to me for energy healing, for whatever problems it may be, must first learn to listen and be patient - this is not magic where someone just place his hand on you and everything is ok.

You need to go to my website and read the healing programme that I have listed then you can understand what to expect. Do not just go to someone blindly just use your judgement see whether it right for you.

It is important not to leave it too late. If money is the issue then how much can you value your life? What is the point if you live the rest of your life in pain and anxiety? To me, my health is my wealth, and it important for me to maintain it until the end.

If you are learning energy work from me I will make sure all students understand exactly how to use it, if not then energy training can cause harm to your body mind and soul.

Many times I have told my students to practise what I have taught them yet there are still some who want to learn from as many masters as possible, each master telling them different ways – this will become more confusing and their level of martial arts and human energy training will become a big mess.

As I always said I am here to send you my message. It is up to each individual to listen and follow, if they choose not to that is their decision. But hopefully I try to make it as clear as possible that I am teaching them for the benefit of everyone and future generations.

Life is unpredictable, one day I might decide not to teach any more.

Sometimes I think that with the way people behave nowadays why should I bother teaching; is there any point? But because I have so many good students around me, who in turn, inspire me with their patience and willing to learn from me then I carry on teaching and will for as long as I can.

I can understand the great sage Lao Tze who left China to become a hermit not wanting to teach any more. Luckily he was stopped by the guard in the border and they begged him to write down his great thinking and philosophy of human living in harmony with nature.

My advice those that are trying to get as many masters as possible, is to stop trying to learn everything, don't be greedy, your body and mind cannot absorb all this information. Stay focused. Most of this information will not be important, rather like downloading too many programmes into a computer and not deleting any unwanted programmes first - it will break down eventually.
You must be patient and practise what I have taught you and eventually you will reach your goal.

The world is full of injustice; the politicians claim to help all these countries with war and poverty but nothing is done. They just sit in their big conference rooms and talk about it and still nothing is done. I just wish they would put the money where their mouth is and do something to help those children, women and elderly refugees in troubled places rather just trying to sell more weapons to these tyrants that rule their country with fear, corruption and oppression toward their people.

For people who keep polluting and destroying Mother Earth, with modern progress and technology, just for our own selfish greed without any concern of others, damaging or hurting people's feeling, and destroying nature.

More and more natural disasters like earthquakes, floods, tornadoes are happening, more frequently and in a much bigger scale - a warning from Mother Earth. All these to me represent bad karma - what goes around comes around. Time will tell and nature will always punish the one who did the bad deed.

This is how I feel nowadays, but what can I do. I am not a politician or a billionaire to voice my opinion and change it in a big way but I believe that maybe by writing this book of mine people will start to take notice. Hopefully there will be some people who read my book and will realise how confused people are nowadays that they just follow everything blindly.

Everyone has their own mind and should use their common sense. For those who have their jobs, home and are financially secure, why should they care? But they should, whatever happens in the world will affect each and everyone living on earth. Therefore collectively we can help to make it better.

I have changed from the first time I arrived in London as a young man of 18 years and naive, full of dreams, thinking I could do anything .

At the age of 28 I had achieved so many of my dreams, like travelling the world, meeting famous people, being a stunt man and bodyguard. It was not how I envisioned my life as a child - I wanted to be a pilot so I could travel the world. Bit I still did it - I did travel everywhere but not as a pilot but as a martial artist.

When I reached my 38th birthday I had taught in so many countries appearing in various TV and movies with my Wing Chun and energy work. It gave me other experiences and teachings too like learning how to handle myself discreetly with the public and in a more caring way; I was starting to grow up by being more patient to others.

At the age of 48, I understood that there are good and bad people everywhere, each individual lives their life differently and I became more patient, more humble and with more tolerance and understanding of people's differences.

Being a master is not just showing how tough you are, but it's also gives you insight and I learnt to teach in a more caring way. Life is not about hurting one another in order to gain respect, but an understanding of give and take with each other and the riches that can bring.

Now I am approaching my 60, I know that I am wiser, like a bottle of fine wine it takes years to achieve maturity. I have grown up; I think that through my knowledge and wisdom learned, cultivated and harnessed over the years, I can properly educate people and pass on my life long experience to the next generation.

People's respect for one another is not born through fear but through learning to understand each other differences, so that we can learn from each other's ways, to better our lives and to be able to live in harmony together.

Anyone who keep the ability to see beauty never grows old.

FINAL THOUGHTS

I can look back through my life with pride always believing in myself, my innovations and ideas, believing strongly in my motto that "action speaks louder than word."

Success is only achieved through hard work, determination and a never say die attitude - this philosophy that makes me achieve my goal and realise my dreams.

I consider myself as a citizen of the world and my heartbeat is the same like everyone else and we should not separate people away from one another but to connect them so that we can all live in harmony.

People should respect one another, it is not through fear but through learning to understand each other's differences so that we can learn from each other's ways to better our lives so that we can live in harmony together.

In my years of experience teaching and healing people all over the world, it has make me realise that all human are the same, each and everyone want the best benefit for themself.

I realise that some people will always be wanting to do more of evcrything like exercises and catching up on lost time, the things because of various commitments in their past that they couldn't do. This thinking is silly as your body needs to slow down if you want a long and healthy life.

Knowledge and wisdom is not always passed on with people who use amazing words and complicated language. It's the simple things like my auntie teaching me the difference between a bed sheet and blankets or my uncle explaining to me how not to put the knife in my mouth while eating. All these things sound trivial but they touched me and these memories will always be with me like my Master's strict teaching, my mum caring for me and of course my grandfather stories all inspire me. All this simple advice it had made me a wiser and better human. What I had received from my Master and Mother Earth has enriched my life. Now I just want to give back to the world my knowledge and energy healing.

Enjoy your moments on earth, take a few steps back, feel the wind and sun on your face and skin, walk along the beach, take deep breaths, let the Chi touch your soul, meditate with nature, feel and listen to your heart beat, then inner peace will be achieved. Embrace your loved ones, feel life as a human being. Life can be cruel too, we cannot stop time but we sure can treasure our past if things go wrong, and when losing our loved ones, our memories and time will help us to heal our body, mind and soul to give us the strength to carry on in life.

Once the book releases I will be in my sixtieth years old. I was told by my Master that according to Chinese Culture, its the right time to received the "Grandmaster" title but to me I still have so much to share with the next generation. My skills, knowledge and experiences over the years would be wasted if I stop teaching and sharing it, so I have decided not to accept this title till I reach my 70th birthday then I will decide.
I hope my Master will understand and accept my decision and thank you again Sifu for taking me so far.

Colours fade, temples crumble, empires fail but wise words remain.

This is my final thought.

CHAPTER 29

Quotes

My Journey

Memories

QUOTES OF THE MASTER

The teacher opens the door, the students have to walk in.

For a longer and healthier life style, one must learn to balance oneself.

Learning all styles does not make you a master. Practising one technique correctly is the first step to becoming a true Master.

Wing Chun is based on close contact fighting.
To master it you must learn to relax in order to achieve speed and power.

Energy healing is not just placing your hands on someone.
You need to learn to understand how the human body works first.
Then it also takes years of training to achieve the healing power.

Being healthy is not just eating healthy food and exercising. You need to maintain a good circulation round your body.

I am just a messenger-my job is to send you my message.

Physical exercise is fine in your younger days Energy training is the only way in your later age.

I am here to pass on my knowledge, skills, philosophy and experience You are not here just to practise punching and kicking only.

MY JOURNEY

Student to Master Level

Bouncer to Bodyguard

First Malaysian Wing Chun Master

Global Martial Arts Teacher

Entrepreneur

TV Star

Hollywood Stuntman

Energy Healer

Author and Publisher

Charity Worker

Inspirationalist

Humanitarian

Naturalist

Man of Tao

Master of Wing Chun

Founder of Human Energy

MEMORIES

STANDING ON RAW EGGS

LION DANCE FOR PRINCESS DIANA

BUTTERFLY KNIVES

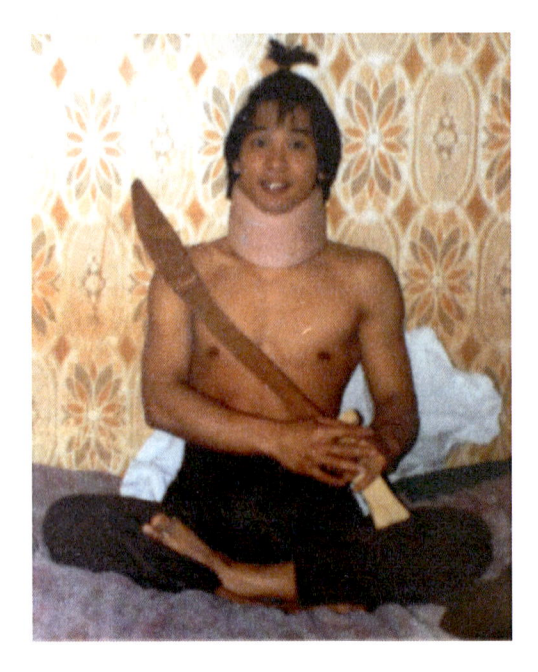

RECOVERING FROM A FRACTURED NECK

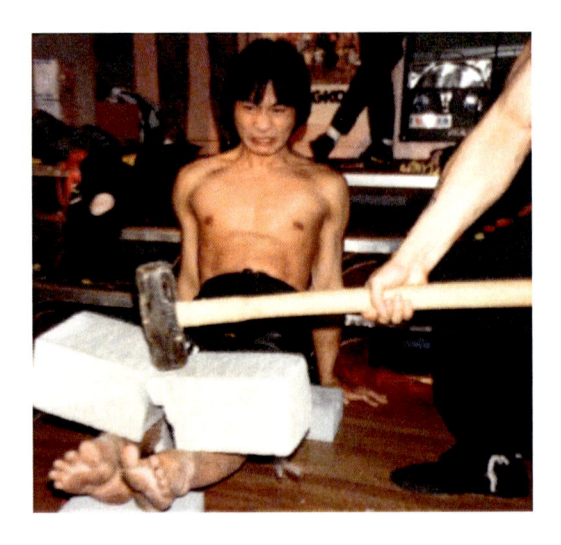

IRON SHIN BONE DEMONSTRATION

TRAINING IN THE SHAOLIN TEMPLE

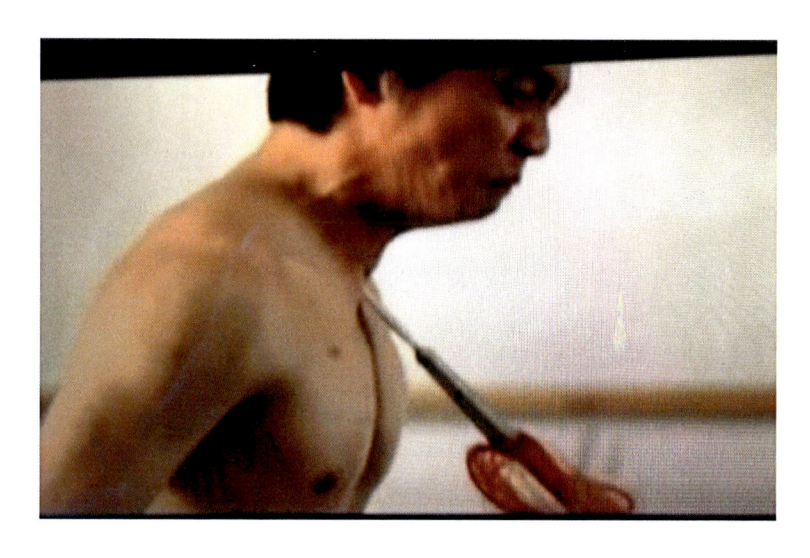

HARD CHI KUNG DEMONSTRATION

The Breaking Power of WING CHUN

By: Master Austin Goh

THROWING CHOPSTICKS DEMONSTRATION

TEACHING IN SAN FRANCISCO

MY FORMAL GYM

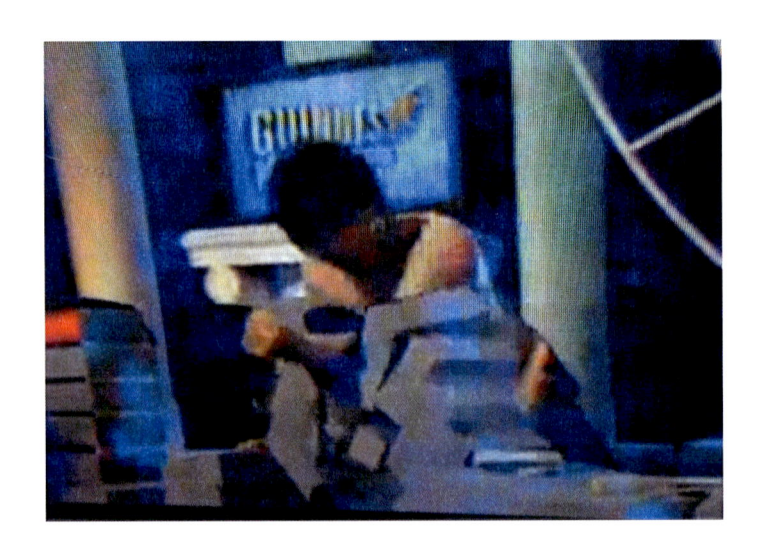

WORLD RECORD IN BREAKING CONCRETE BLOCKS

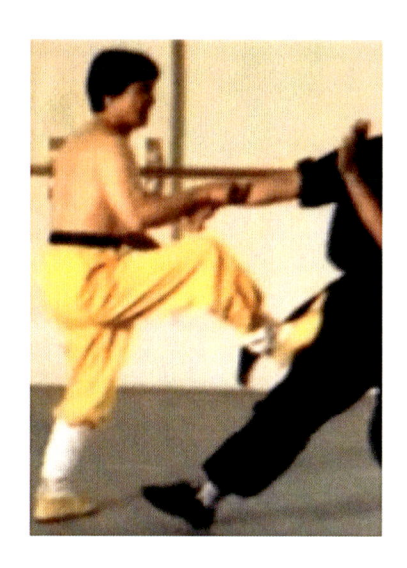

SPARRING

IRON STOMACH DEMONSTRATION

POWER TRAINING

HOLLYWOOD STUNTWORK

ALWAYS IN TOP CONDITION

ENERGY MASTER

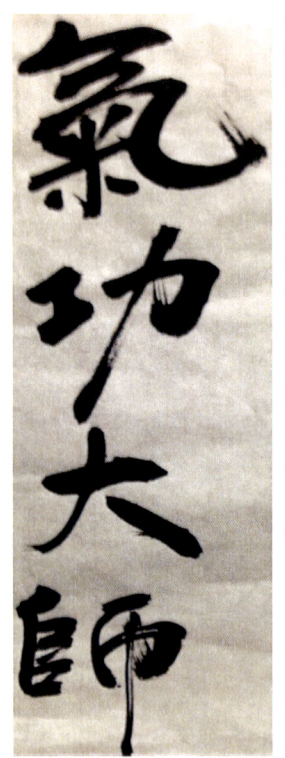

氣功大師

DESCENDANT OF WING CHUN

詠春傳人

Thank you for taking the time to read a small part of my memoir, May my Chi always be with you.

This book was written so that I can share my life journey, arts and philosophy with you. I always like to hear from my students around the world, if you have any questions or feedback please email me at info@austingoh.com

Empty Your Mind

TAO

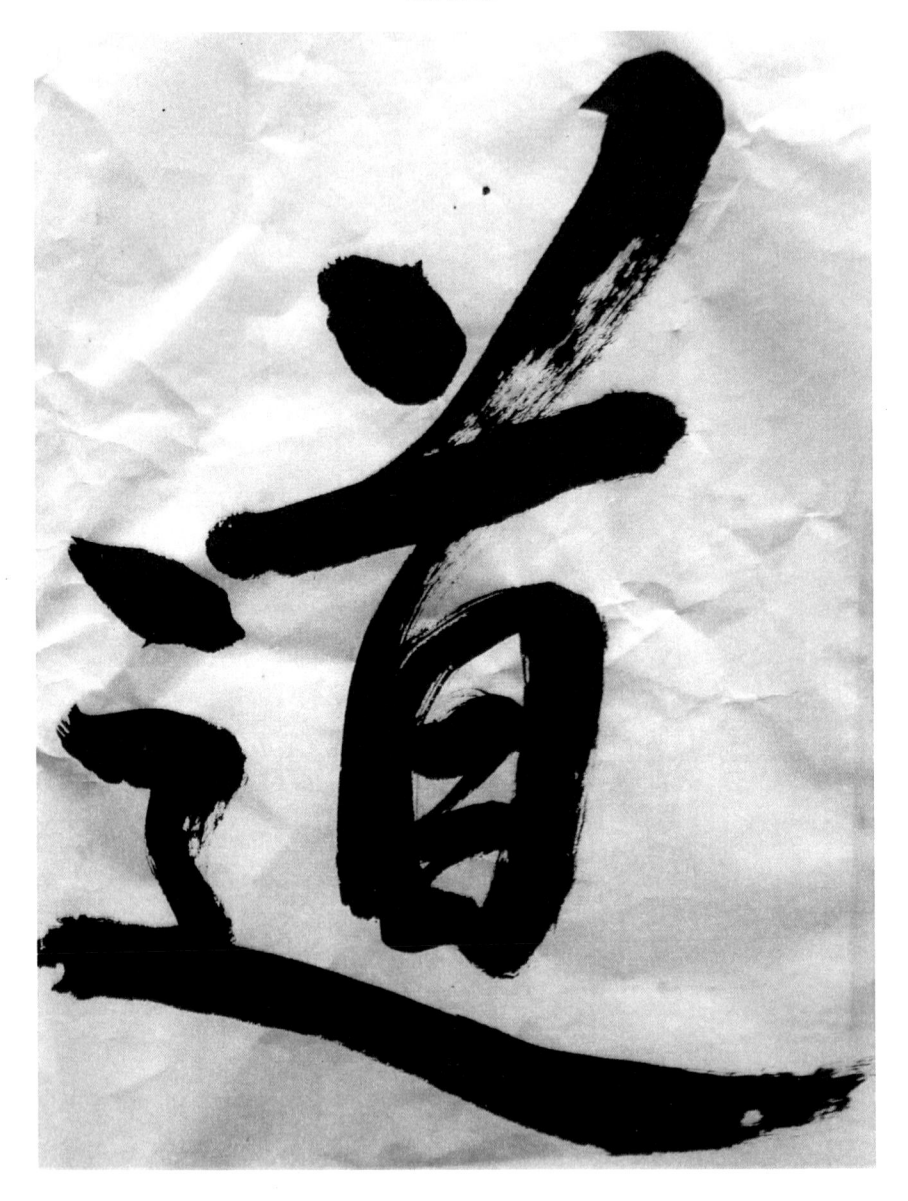

Is the way to unity of humans and nature